Humanism
and Capitalism

Humanism
and Capitalism
A Survey of
Thought on Morality
Bernard Murchland

Library of Congress Cataloging in Publication Data

Murchland, Bernard.
    Humanism and capitalism.

    (AEI studies; 387)
      1. Economics—Moral and ethical aspects.
2. Capitalism—Moral and ethical aspects. 3. Humanism.
I. Title.
HB72.M79   1983   174   83-11785
ISBN 0-8447-3529-9

AEI Studies 387

Printed in the United States of America

The literary world then agreed that truth survived in Germany alone, and Carlyle, Matthew Arnold, Renan, Emerson, with scores of popular followers taught the German faith.
—HENRY ADAMS

An enormous majority of Western intellectuals display and affirm hostility to the economic and social institutions of their society, institutions to which they give the blanket name of capitalism. —BERTRAND DE JOUVENEL

Contents

Foreword

Modern commercial culture has created economic growth and prosperity unprecedented in the history of mankind. This is a remarkable achievement. More than any other form of political economy, democratic capitalism would seem to have borne important humanistic fruits, not only in its immense creativity in economics but in an unprecedented flowering of the arts and sciences.

Nonetheless, many humanists of the nineteenth and early twentieth century seemed to hold as a commonplace that humanism and commerce are antagonists. Most of them more or less abandoned reflection on the economic system to economists and on the political system to political scientists and practitioners. Important philosophical and ethical issues at the base of democratic capitalism have been neglected. Yet democratic capitalism, like any other system of political economy, generates a powerful moral and cultural system—in this case, one that is pluralistic, free, and turbulent.

With the publication of *Humanism and Capitalism,* the American Enterprise Institute hopes to encourage a more fruitful dialogue between humanists and those involved in reflection upon economic activity, from which will emerge, it is hoped, a more critical, comprehensive humanism, open to the full range of humankind's creative capacities.

This study is another in a series published under the guidance of AEI's Center for Religion, Philosophy, and Public Policy. Under the direction of resident scholar Michael Novak, the Center has pioneered in examining the moral, religious, and cultural dimensions of political economy and in analyzing their role in current debates on public policy.

WILLIAM J. BAROODY, JR.
President
American Enterprise Institute

Preface

In 1922 Harold E. Stearns edited a volume entitled *Civilization in the United States*. The entry on business was written by Garet Garrett, a financial writer for several New York newspapers, including the *Wall Street Journal*.

Garrett began his essay by asserting that modern business derives from three passions: the passion for things, the passion for personal grandeur, and the passion for power. Addressing the question of "morality" in business, he stated bluntly that it is a term without meaning. Business, he said, "is neither moral nor immoral. It represents man's acquisitive instinct acting outside of humanistic motives."[1]

When I read Garrett's essay some ten years ago I thought his judgment of business somewhat extreme but essentially sound, for I too was a humanist to whom all things commercial were foreign. By the time I finished research for this study I realized that Garrett's position was not extreme but typical. And I concluded that it was not sound but fundamentally fallacious. Modern humanists have not on the whole been open to the full range of experience. They have tended to be narrow, elitist, and abstract, and they are virtually unanimous in their rejection of commercial culture.

Why is this?

We are accustomed to attacks on capitalism from socialists. Indeed, we sometimes have the impression that their sole function is to attack capitalism. But the humanist critics of capitalism were mostly conservatives, even arch-conservatives. So we are confronted with the phenomenon of commercial culture being attacked from both the left and the right. Often the criticisms are remarkably similar.

This is not so strange when we stop to think about it. Conservative humanists and socialists feed on a common stock of premodern values. To that extent, both are reactionary. For example, the conservative doctrine of the divine right of kings (going back to Plato) is not so different from the collectivist bent of the socialists. This may explain why socialism today appeals primarily to feudal societies.

In both cases a strong central power is postulated as the imposer of rational order and the enforcer of morals. Both conservatives and socialists see themselves as illuminati, possessed of special knowledge that entitles them to run things. Put another way, both conservatives and socialists see the liberal state, of which capitalism is an integral part, as the enemy. Their criticism of this order is, I believe, radically flawed because they rely excessively on premodern canons of criticism.

1. Garet Garrett, "Business," in *Civilization in the United States: An Inquiry by Thirty Americans,* ed. Harold E. Stearns (New York: Harcourt, Brace, 1922), p. 410.

1
Two Humanisms:
England Divided against Itself

By one of history's great coincidences, idealism in Germany reached its most intense pitch just as capitalism was enjoying a rapid first growth in England. German philosophy thus provided a ready-made weapon to the English critics of the new economic order. To explore the reasons why English humanists were attracted to idealism, what ideas they adapted to their critical purposes and with what results, is to go quite some distance in clarifying a longstanding conflict between humanism and capitalism.

One may wonder that so foreign a philosophy should take deep root or have much influence on British soil. But one must remember that the England of the late eighteenth and early nineteenth centuries was a rapidly evolving country. George III came to the throne in 1760. During his reign, which ended in 1820, the French and American revolutions took place, industry and technology made major strides, great political reforms were instituted, the French War of 1793–1797 was fought, Ireland was perennially restive, and a protracted war with Napoleon was waged between 1803 and 1815— events that could strain a far more robust constitution than George III possessed.

The England of this time was complex and, in many serious ways, divided against itself. It was rationalistic and empirical, but there were strong strains of imagination and mysticism as well. Industry progressed side by side with lasting feudal structures. Religion thrived even as secularism and atheism advanced. Classicism and romanticism vied with each other for cultural ascendancy. This England was in effect a battleground between two humanisms. One, in a line that might be traced from Francis Bacon through John Locke and Adam Smith to Jeremy Bentham and John Stuart Mill, favored the modern developments of science, democracy, and capitalism. The other humanism followed a primarily literary-religious track, beginning with Renaissance humanists like Petrarch and Erasmus—the great opposers—and continuing in an unbroken line through the German idealists to Carlyle, Ruskin, and Matthew Arnold. This brand of humanism set itself against modernism and in particular, with deadly determination, against the new economic and industrial civilization that was emerging.

The ground for the influx of German idealism was well prepared by religious revivals among the Methodists and the Quakers, by a new social consciousness embodied in Chartism and the Owenites, and by the literary protest of radical poets like William Blake and William Cowper, culminating in 1789 with the publication of that powerful Romantic manifesto *Lyrical Ballads*, by Samuel Taylor Coleridge and William Wordsworth. Elements of idealism were incorporated in much of this, either directly as in Coleridge's work or indirectly as in the frequent evocations of nature or of the Middle Ages. The Middle Ages were frequently regarded as a time of robust faith and charming simplicity. Nature, as in Wordsworth's poetry, is wrapped in the symbols of divinity.[1]

Thomas Carlyle: Drinking Deeply at the Sources

No one drank more deeply at the German sources than did Thomas Carlyle. From Kant and Schelling, from Novalis and Schiller, above all from Goethe and Fichte, he became familiar with expansive ideas about hidden harmonies and the spiritual radiance of the world, about the organic bonds that unite societies, and about the role of the hero in history. He learned that all reality is spiritual ("the world is a vesture of spirit") and that men (some men) are endowed with higher mental faculties with which to grasp this reality.[2] Armed with these ideas Carlyle took up cudgels against empiricism and scepticism, against materialism and unbelief, against commerce and democracy. He became, according to some, the greatest moral force of his day, a social critic comparable to Marx.

The new industrial order is the focus of Carlyle's attack. He abominates laissez-faire economics; he is no less scornful of democracy. His voice is never less than strident. In *Past and Present* one can read, more or less at random, passages such as "Laissez-faire, Supply-and-demand, —one begins to be weary of all that. Leave all to egoism, to ravenous greed of money, of pleasure, of applause: —it is the Gospel of Despair!"[3] Or, in a blast against the Manchester Chamber of Commerce:

> Supply-and-demand, —alas! Ah me, into what waste latitudes, in this Time-Voyage, have we wandered: like adventurous Sindbads: —where the men go about as if by galvanism, with meaningless eyes, and have no soul, but

only a beaver-faculty and stomach! The haggard-despair of the Cotton-factory, Coal-mine operatives, Chandos Farm-labourers, in these days, is painful to behold; but not so painful, hideous to the inner sense, as that brutish god-forgetting Profit-and-Loss Philosophy and life-theory, which we hear jangled on all hands of us . . . as the Ultimate Gospel and candid Plain-English of Man's Life.[4]

In "Chartism" industry is decried:

The huge demon of Mechanism smokes and thunders, pant-ing at his great task, in all sections of the English land; changing his shape like a very Proteus; and infallibly, at every change of shape, oversetting whole multitudes of workmen, and as if with the waving of his shadow from afar, hurtling them asunder, this way and that, in their crowded march and course of work or traffic; so that the wisest no longer knows his whereabout.[5]

Bad as the outward effect of industry on workers is, this of itself does not constitute their chief misery, which stems, rather, from the feeling of injustice. Economic laissez faire may cause poverty; but political laissez faire, that is, democracy, brings about injustice. Carlyle considers political laissez faire an abdication on the part of governors, an admission that they are henceforward incompetent to rule.[6] This constitutes an inversion of his conception of the universe as a monarchy. Carlyle envisages the masses as dumb creatures crying out in rage and pain to be guided:

Surely, of all rights of man, this right of the ignorant man to be guided by the wiser, to be, gently or forcibly, held in the true course by him, is the indisputablest. Nature herself ordains it from the first; Society struggles toward perfection by enforcing and accomplishing it more and more. If Free-dom have any meaning, it means enjoyment of this right, wherein all other rights are enjoyed.[7]

Democracy contradicts the order of nature and therefore denies men their "indisputablest" of rights. In democracy can "lie no finality . . . with the completest winning of democracy there is nothing yet won, —except emptiness, and the free chance to win! Democracy is, by the nature of it, a self-cancelling business; and gives in the long run a net result of *zero*. . . . Democracy never yet, that we heard of, was able to accomplish much work, beyond that same cancelling of itself."[8] Democracy abrogates the old order and leaves nothing in its place but "the consummation of No-government and Laissez-faire." Carlyle formulates what he believes to be a better ideal:

Cannot one discern too, across all democratic turbulence, clattering of ballot boxes and infinite sorrowful jungle, needful or not, that this at bottom is the wish and prayer of all human hearts, everywhere and at all times: 'Give me a leader; a true leader, not a false sham-leader; a true leader, that he may guide me on the true way, that I may be loyal to him, that I may swear fealty to him and follow him, and feel that it is well with me!' The relation of the taught to their teacher, of the loyal subject to his guiding king, is under one shape or another, the vital element of human society.[9]

Carlyle is repetitious and soon grows tedious, but there is a punchy, abandoned quality to his prose that gives it a certain charm even for modern readers. He lets the scattershot of his rhetoric fall where it may, but the underlying theme is a lament for an age that is rapidly passing. God's laws, Carlyle says, have become moral laws "sanctioned by able computations" of profit and loss. The principle of greatest happiness, the moral maxim of the utilitarians, and parliamentary expedience have blinded men to "the eternal substance of things." He detects no reflection of nature's laws in the marketplace or the senate house, in the cathedral or the circulating library. The Gospel of Mammonism reigns supreme, and hell has become the fear of not making money. What a singular hell! Carlyle exclaims. In sum, laissez faire is "the shabbiest Gospel ever preached" because it has replaced organic social bonds with purely mechanical ones; leaving cash payment as the sole nexus between man and man. Actually, Carlyle's position has a certain logic to it: if capitalism claims to satisfy all human needs by reducing them to purely monetary ones, then it stands condemned if human nature has other needs. His error is in supposing that capitalism claimed to satisfy all human needs. The idealist is prone to expect of one realm of society what only the whole society can provide.

Carlyle begins "Shooting Niagara" with the mournful observation that the rising tide of democracy, atheism, and free trade has not been stemmed by his more than thirty years of criticism. There is a sentiment of failure in these pages: society has grown palpably more rotten; people are in a state of mouldering decay, desirous of nothing but making money. But Carlyle is still resolved to bring a nefarious age to the rule and square of prophetic judgment. He saw no good coming from the American Civil War since "the Nigger was appointed by the Almighty Maker to be a servant."[10] He could muster no enthusiasm for the Reform Bill of 1867, acidly remarking: "Inexpressibly delirious seems to me . . . the calling in of new supplies of blockheadism, gullibility, bribeability, amenability to beer and balderdash by way of amending the woes we have had from our previous supplies of that bad article." And then the turn of the screw: "The intellect of a man who believes in the possibility of improvement by such a method is to me a finished-off and shut-up intellect, with which I would not argue."[11]

Whether or not it be true that Carlyle is "unequaled in the 19th century as a critic of the social effects of individualism, of the profit-gain system,"[12] it is clear that his proposed solutions bordered on the fanciful. He made some specific suggestions concerning, for example, education and the reform of labor. But he placed his greatest hope in the leadership of great men, in "the Noble Few on whom and whose living of a noble and valiantly cosmic life amid the worst impediments and hugest anarchies, the whole of our hope depends."[13] An aristocracy formed of the best of the old nobility and the new captains of industry (a rather odd concession to capitalism) were to be the new hero-kings who would create "a noble industrialism and Government by the Wisest." To them would fall the task of regimenting the workers like soldiers, putting order in the place of chaos, and recovering the lost traces of divinity in the world. Carlyle's social criticism was no doubt amusing—though perhaps instructive—to his contemporaries, but it was even then reactionary and can only appear somewhat ludicrous to us today. As it turned out, capitalism did far more for the workers than Carlyle's chilling blueprint ever could have. There were indeed abuses in the new industrial order, but they could not compare with the horrors that would have resulted from Carlyle's ideas, for they lead by the directest of paths to fascism. It is hard to believe that he cared about the workers as much as about his ideas concerning them.

One of the keener insights that can be gleaned from Carlyle's social criticism (especially if we read carefully between the lines) is that the condition of England results more from inept government than from capitalism. As the historian David Harris Willson puts it: "The years since 1789 had been years of profound economic and social change, but the government, intent on war, had done nothing to guide the forces of industrial development and rapid urbanization." Most of England's institutions, he adds,

> devised in an earlier and simpler age, were inadequate for the complex problems of the 19th century; the poor law was Elizabethan; so was the church, which, with its many abuses, its badly distributed revenues, and its neglect of the urban poor, had not been overhauled since the Tudor period; the Acts of Trade, a product of the 17th century, were still in

5

force; the universities and the Inns of Court were just awakening from their 18th century slumbers; the law was in great need of reform; there was an exaggerated respect for the rights of property and vested interest. England might boast of her constitution, but in truth she was inefficiently governed by a small landed aristocracy whose standard of conduct, both in public service and in private morals, was not high.[14]

Obsolete laws and the political prejudices of the nobles against democracy and commerce were the principal causes of suffering among the workers and the poor. The times called for political reform. Carlyle was not oblivious to this point, but the kind of reform he had in mind could only have made matters worse.

John Ruskin: The Golden Side of Humanity

John Ruskin was Carlyle's greatest disciple and was a major figure in the development of socialism in England. He declared himself to be a "communist of the old school"—which is to say, one who believes that everyone must work in common and that public property must be "more and statelier in all its substance" than private property. Like his master, Ruskin believed that the masses are inferior, that the profit motive is corrupting, and that materialism is the great social sin. He also held a Platonic view of justice according to which society is an organic, closely knit hierarchy of bonded ranks. To this Ruskin adds an aesthetic criticism: industrialism is to be condemned because it makes ugly the cities and the countryside. Beauty is a moral ideal. No sensitive spirit, he thought, could live in London or any other industrial city.

Unto This Last, a basic statement of Ruskin's political philosophy, begins with an attack on the political economists (he has in mind particularly John Stuart Mill). He objects essentially to their truncated view of human nature. They peel away the flesh and deal abstractly and mechanically with the skeleton. They recognize avarice and desire for progress among human motives but ignore other qualities such as the affections and intellectual and moral goods. Human actions, says Ruskin, should be guided by the balance of justice rather than by expediency. Because the economists fail to see this they have produced nothing but an "ossifiant theory of progress" founded upon the exclusion of important human attributes. The soldier, the pastor, the physician, the lawyer, and the merchant represent the five great vocations necessary to civilized life. Each of these upon "due occasion" must be prepared to die for his honor.

What is the "due occasion" of the merchant's death? When he fails in his engagements and when he puts the profit motive over the excellence of products. A merchant should regard profits as a clergyman his stipend: incidental to his main purpose of rendering service.[15]

In a letter in 1862 Ruskin states his position in these words:

> The Science of Political Economy is a lie—wholly and to the very root (as hitherto taught). It is also the damnedest—that is to say, the most utterly and to the lowest pit condemned of God and his Angels—that the Devil, or Betrayer of Men, has yet invented, except his (the Devil's) theory of Sanctification. To this "Science" and to this alone (the professed and organized pursuit of Money) is owing *All* the evil of modern days. I say All. The Monastic Theory is at an end. It is now the Money theory which corrupts the Church, corrupts the household life, destroys honour, beauty, and life throughout the universe. It is *the* Death incarnate of Modernism, and the so-called science of its pursuit is the most cretinous, speechless, paralysing plague that has yet touched the brains of mankind.[16]

In *Unto This Last* Ruskin argues that riches are "a power like that of electricity, acting only through inequalities or negations of itself."[17] To make oneself rich is "equally and necessarily" to keep one's neighbor poor. True economy for Ruskin is the production and distribution of useful and pleasurable things that add to the wealth and well-being of society. In one of his common formulations, wealth is what conduces to life. But that is not possible under capitalism where the economy comes to mean the accumulation of wealth and power by a few individuals. He is careful to point out the close connection between wealth and power. "What is really desired under the name of riches, is, essentially, power over men."[18] Since this power is greater in proportion to the poverty of those over whom it is exercised, the art of growing rich becomes the art of "establishing the maximum inequality."

Thus there can be no just wage under capitalism. The principle of exchange decrees that profits must always deprive the poor; the law of supply and demand inevitably brings about inequality. In practice, he says, "according to the laws of demand and supply, when two men are ready to do the work, and only one man wants to have it done, the two men underbid each other for it; and the one who gets it to do is underpaid. But when two men want the work done, and there is only one man ready to do it, the two men who want it done overbid each other, and the workman is overpaid."[19] According to Ruskin, one of the follies of the political economists is to imagine

7

that such inequalities are advantageous to society or that they are "natural." He compares the circulation of wealth to that of blood. When the organism of society is healthy, the flow is quick and wholesome; when it is feverish, the flow will turn to putrefaction. The touted virtues of political economy—materialism, competition, self-interest, the monetary standard of value—were for Ruskin moral defects. Therefore, what the political economists overlook is the moral aspect of wealth. The real value of wealth, Ruskin writes, "depends on the moral sign attached to it, just as sternly as that of a mathematical quantity depends on the algebraical sign attached to it."[20] Nothing is more "insolently futile" than talking about wealth while ignoring its moral dimension.

When this fuller moral vision is taken into account, production will be judged according to consumption, and consumption will be judged according to life needs. Whence Ruskin's great principle: there is no wealth but life! That country is richest, he says, "which nourishes the greatest number of noble and happy human beings; that man is richest who, having perfected the functions of his own life to the utmost, has also the widest helpful influence, both personal, and by means of his possessions, over the lives of others."[21] By this line of reasoning, Ruskin denies the claim that self-interest is the basis of political economy.

Again like Carlyle, Ruskin sees in America the tenets of political economy run amuck. There the laws of supply and demand operate unhindered. And what have they wrought? "Lust of wealth, and trust in it; vulgar faith in magnitude and multitude, instead of nobleness . . . perpetual self-contemplation issuing in passionate vanity and total ignorance of the finer and higher arts."[22] In one of his vignettes, Ruskin tells of riding from Venice to Verona with an American family recently come into much wealth. The two teen-age girls, he notes, had been indulged in everything. They had everything money could buy, yet they had no eye for or interest in the many delightful sights along the way: neither Portia's villa, Juliet's tomb, Petrarch's home, nor the Alps in the summer sunshine. This epitomized for Ruskin the failure of industrial civilization: it kills the finer sensibilities.

Despite his overstatement and bombast, Ruskin at his best was an able critic. He was well versed in the literature of the political economists and saw obvious weaknesses in the fledgling capitalist system (though many of them appeared more harmful than they turned out to be). Some of his suggestions for reform are worthy of attention. By introducing the functional view of property and vital value as an economic concept, he was to have a major influence on such later guild socialists as J. A. Hobson and R. H. Tawney. But his social criticism is a case of being right in many small ways but wrong in some rather large ones. I cite three examples.

The first is his pervasive aestheticism. Ruskin came to economics by way of art criticism, and he persistently confused the one with the other—"confused" in the literal sense of fusing the two without distinction. The story about the American girls reveals this confusion of realms. Ruskin reasons that because they are rich but ignorant of aesthetics, their wealth must be the cause of their ignorance. This is the elementary logical fallacy of *post hoc, ergo propter hoc*. Many poor American girls were no doubt equally ignorant, though Ruskin would not have been likely to meet them in Italy. It is puzzling that he did not make more of the aesthetic aspects of capitalism or see in the game of money (as he often referred to it) a valid expression of our fiction-making capacities. In any event, while aesthetic considerations can be relevant to economics, it is unfair as well as wrongheaded to ask that an economic order fulfill all our longings for grace and beauty. Work is not aesthetics; morality is not art. Ruskin blamed capitalism for failures that were in fact failures of the moral-cultural realm. One is often caught up beautifully in his writing style— studded as it is with quotations from the Latin and Greek and with sumptuous literary allusions. But it is not a style well calculated to hold our minds to the social and economic issues Ruskin wanted to emphasize.

A second weakness in Ruskin's social criticism is his pervasive feudalism. He often contradicted himself by calling for economic equality but denying political equality. He rejected democracy categorically. He proclaimed himself illiberal, considered freedom "error," and condemned the opinions of the mass of men. One is astounded to hear him assert that slavery is "an inherent, natural and eternal inheritance of a large portion of the human race—to whom, the more you give of their own free will, the more slaves they will make themselves."[23] How, one wants to ask, is this slavery superior to capitalism? And how, in this state, can all things be held in common? Ruskin follows Plato and Carlyle in defending an autocracy of the upper classes. He envisaged a society built along feudal lines of more or less fixed class ranks, with a king standing at the top and a large body of workers at the bottom. In the end, the workers function in this scheme as little more than children. How, therefore, can such a class be capable of "creative workmanship"? It is one thing that Ruskin failed to grasp freedom as a political virtue; that he failed to see it as a necessary condition for creativity is incomprehensible.

The third weakness of Ruskin's social criticism is his idealism, by which he was, finally, betrayed. He approached the shield of humanity, to use Wordsworth's image, always from the golden side. He thought it the better part of realism to appeal to man's higher instincts and persisted in the belief that human nature is basically generous and kind. But why would good men voluntarily submit to the direction of their "true masters"? Ruskin wanted a new heaven and a new earth, with all former things passed away. But his political recommendations were scarcely new; they date from the primitive origins of the race. Not surprisingly, Ruskin's major venture into applied socialism, the founding of the Companions of St. George in 1878, was a disaster. Even Carlyle thought it laughable. The rich, to Ruskin's amazement, were reluctant to contribute to his cause; membership was sparse; leadership was lacking. Numerous contretemps brought about the dissolution of the guild not long after it was founded, and Ruskin drifted into a nescient senility that lasted for some ten years, until his death in 1900.

Matthew Arnold: Upward toward Sweetness and Light

Matthew Arnold is the third member of a triumvirate that constitutes the mainstream of anticapitalist humanism in nineteenth-century England. He, too, was directly influenced by "the puissant voice of Carlyle" and praised his Oxford master for introducing him to Goethe, whom he considered the greatest voice of the century. The familiar charges against materialism, laissez faire, and individualism ring through his writings. He advocates an organic view of society and adopted much of Ruskin's aestheticism. Like Ruskin, he deplored the ugly towns and cities created by industrialism. Arnold also shares with Carlyle and Ruskin a melancholic temperament. What he called "the strange disease of modern life" seems often to be a projection of his morbid imagination. Although he remained suspicious of the masses—his aristocratic sympathies ran deep—Arnold was nonetheless a defender of democracy, which distinguishes him from his two compeers. It was, in fact, his defense of democracy that led him to criticize capitalism.

In his essay "Democracy" (1861), Arnold acknowledged that the aristocracy could no longer continue to govern England. Democracy, for multiple reasons, was inevitable, an idea whose time had come.[24] Democracy, he wrote grandiosely, is like life itself in wanting "to affirm its own essence." He saw it as a "movement of nature" that had been growing ever since Europe emerged from barbarism.

> Life itself consists, say the philosophers, in the effort *to affirm one's own essence*; meaning by this, to develop one's own existence fully and freely, to have ample light and air,

to be neither cramped nor overshadowed. Democracy is trying to *affirm its own essence;* to live, to enjoy, to possess the world, as aristocracy has tried, and successfully tried, before it.[25]

The essence of democracy is equality; that is why it is opposed by so many people. Yet can anyone deny, Arnold asks, "that to live in a society of equals tends in general to make a man's spirits expand and his faculties work easily and actively"?[26] And, conversely, living in an aristocracy, while it may be good discipline, tends to have the opposite effect and "tame the spirits." Arnold provides generously for state action, well realizing that the state is the great ally of middle-class interests. The state is, he often said echoing Edmund Burke, the organ of our collective best selves. "With all the force I can, I wish to urge upon the middle classes of this country, both that they might be very greatly profited by the action of the State, and also that they are continuing their opposition to such action out of an unfounded fear."[27]

Arnold develops these notions further in his 1879 essay, "Equality," which takes the form of a long exegesis of a fragment from Menander: Choose equality and flee greed. He begins by taking cognizance of the many objections raised against equality by his contemporaries. William Gladstone, for example, had said that no idea was more foreign to the English political system than the love of equality. Arnold takes the high road by making the argument for equality also the argument for culture. The case for the one goes hand in hand with the case for the other. "A community with a spirit of society is eminently, therefore, a community with the spirit of equality. A nation with a genius for society, like the French or the Athenians, is irresistibly drawn toward equality."[28] Throughout the essay Arnold is inordinately lavish in his praise of the French. No one better than they, he maintains, has brought culture and equality together in a successful political experiment. In France the people are most human because most civilized.

England is far less fortunate. In *Culture and Anarchy* Arnold at length lamented the class division of barbarians, philistines, and populace, "three distinct and unfused bodies." There was, wrote Arnold, too much luxury at the top, too much seriousness in the middle, and too much squalor at the bottom. There seemed to be no way in such a structure to affirm a common human element, an informing *geist.* Why are the English so uncivilized? Because, Arnold answers, of inequality. England suffers by comparison with France. And what causes inequality? The blame is laid squarely on materialism. Surely it is easy to see, Arnold writes, that our shortcomings in civilization are due to our inequality; or, in other words, that the great inequality of classes and property, which came to us from the Middle Age and which we maintain because we have the religion of inequality, that this constitution of things, I say, has the natural and necessary effect, under present circumstances, of materializing the upper class, vulgarizing our middle class, and brutalizing our lower class. And this is to fail in civilization.[29]

The strong mental links Arnold forges between the terms "barbarism," "inequality," and "materialism" give him his angle of attack on capitalism.

Arnold shares with Ruskin the idea that the purpose of culture is to produce great numbers of rational, happy people. But the middle class becomes a stumbling block to this ideal; their energies are drained away in the making of money. "The fineness and capacity of a man's spirit is shown by his enjoyments; your middle class has an enjoyment in its business, we admit, and gets on well in business, and makes money; but beyond that? Drugged with business, your middle class seems to have its sense blunted for any stimulus besides. . . ."[30] The aim of politics is to promote civilization, that is, the humanization of man in society, the elevation of a whole people to culture. Arnold saw all political and economic problems through his root metaphor of a humanity struggling ever upwards toward sweetness and light. This high-mindedness sometimes makes him sound as though social problems were the result of bad taste.

The middle class cannot take over the role of leadership abandoned by a self-indulgent and effete aristocracy until they measure up to Arnold's cultural requirements. In its heyday the old aristocracy was "bottomed on vital ideas and sentiments," which made it tough and resilient; the middle class is too bent on getting rich and too individualistic to rise to this standard. There is a woeful lack of spirit in its doings. The middle class has "no great, seriously and truly conceived end; —therefore no greatness of soul or mind; —therefore no steadfastness and power in great affairs."[31] Arnold exhorts the middle class to "search and not rest till it sees things more as they really are, and how little of a power over things as they really are is its money-making."[32]

One of Arnold's clearest statements of social criticism appears in his 1882 essay, "The Future of Liberalism." There he observes that the Liberals have prospered politically by cleverly linking the notions of trade and liberty. The mass of the community, he writes, "sees in the Liberals the friends of trade as well as the friends of liberty."[33] Arnold does not deny the connection between trade and liberty, but it is far from meeting his sense of what a cultural ideal should be. He states his position on this question in these words: "For we have working in us, as elements towards civilization, besides the instinct for expansion, the instinct also . . . for conduct, the instinct for intellect and knowledge, the instinct for beauty, the instinct for a fit and pleasing form of social life and manners."[34]

The liberal order, despite its political freedoms and its supremacy of trade and industry, does not satisfy these larger instincts. Indeed, under industrialism they find "uneasiness and stoppage." The philistine middle class to which the Liberal politicians make appeal is, then, narrow in its range of intellect and knowledge, is stunted in its sense of beauty and dignity, has a low standard of social life and manners, and is ignorant of all of these deficiencies. Arnold calls special attention to beauty as a basic human instinct. The Conservatives do somewhat better than the Liberals do in meeting this cultural standard, but in the end they too fail to satisfy the total needs of the community.

Arnold, in "The Future of Liberalism," returns to the problem of equality. Industrialism, he believes, promotes inequality. "Whenever there is an immense inequality of conditions and property, such inequality inevitably depresses and degrades the inferior masses."[35] Manufacturers call forth large numbers of workers to places like St. Helens, Wigan, and Bolton, but when demand slackens they are abandoned. In this way capitalists grow rich while the workers are left to fortune. In this demoralizing seesaw, Arnold points out, people discover that free political institutions do not guarantee either economic well-being or equality. Yet equality is a human need as important as any other.

> Not until this need to which they appeal . . . is better understood by Liberal statesmen, is understood to include equality as well as political liberty and free trade, —and is cared for by them, yet cared for not singly and exorbitantly, but in union and proportion with the progress of man in conduct, and his growth in intellect and knowledge, and his near approach to beauty and manners, —will Liberal governments be secure.[36]

Arnold's loyalties are with the Liberals. Nevertheless, he will not support them, nor indeed does he think they will survive, until they understand that the aim of the true politician is to promote the highest ends of culture. This is what civilization means. It may be, Arnold admits, an ideal laid away in a Platonic heaven, but only by such ideals can we judge the progress of civilization. By that measure, capitalism falls far short.

Notes

1. Nicholas A. H. Stacey has argued that women novelists played a major role in creating anticapitalist attitudes in England. The real reason for their animosity, Stacey writes, was dislike of the nouveau riche by the establishment. "Only furious, unfettered social dislike can validate the consensus of condemnation echoed by 'the condition of England' novelists in the late 18th century. I have no shadow of doubt that the early women novelists were influential in casting the first cloud over the achievements of the industrial age. Writers of a later age, including such celebrated novelists as Benjamin Disraeli, were influenced by them and published books which too condemned the commercial, anti-aristocratic state of England in political terms and endeavoured to establish a type of idyllic, romantic new Toryism." Stacey mentions such novelists as Harriet Martineau, Elizabeth Gaskell, Frances Trollope, Susan Ferrier, George Eliot, and Emily Eden in his "The Sociology of the Entrepreneur" (Paper delivered at McMaster's University, Hamilton, Ontario, 1980).

2. A good analysis of Carlyle's indebtedness to the Germans can be found in Charles F. Harrold, *Carlyle and German Thought, 1819–1834* (New Haven, Conn.: Yale University Press, 1934).

3. Thomas Carlyle, *Past and Present* (New York: AMS Press, 1969), p. 184. The principal sources of Carlyle's social criticism are his early *Signs of the Times* (1829) and *Characteristics* (1831). His views are amplified in "Chartism" (1839), *Past and Present* (1843), and "Shooting Niagara" (1867).

4. Ibid., pp. 186–87.

5. Thomas Carlyle, "Chartism," in *Critical and Miscellaneous Essays*, vol. 4 (New York: AMS Press, 1969), pp. 141–42.

6. Ibid., p. 156.

7. Ibid., pp. 157–58.

8. Ibid., p. 158. The American experiment was proof positive for Carlyle that democracy was an abominable political system. In *Latter-Day Pamphlets* he wrote: "What great human soul, what great thought, what great noble thing that one could worship, or loyally admire, has yet been produced there? What have they done? They have doubled their population every twenty years. They have begotten, with a rapidity beyond recorded example, Eighteen Millions of the greatest bores ever seen in this world before, that hitherto is their feat in History." Thomas Carlyle, *Latter-Day Pamphlets* (London: Chapman and Hall, 1853), p. 18.

9. Ibid., pp. 159–60.

10. Thomas Carlyle, "Shooting Niagara," in *Critical and Miscellaneous Essays*, vol. 5 (New York: AMS Press, 1969), p. 5.

11. Ibid., p. 9.

12. B. E. Lippincott, *Victorian Critics of Democracy* (Minneapolis: University of Minnesota Press, 1938), p. 18.

13. Carlyle, "Shooting Niagara," p. 21.

14. David Harris Willson, *A History of England*, 2d ed. (Hinsdale, Ill.: Dryden Press, 1972), pp. 581–82.

15. See John Ruskin, *Unto This Last: Four Essays on the First Principles of Political Economy* (New York: Thomas Y. Crowell and Co., 1901), pp. 30ff.

16. Quoted in Holbrook Jackson, *Dreamers of Dreams: The Rise and Fall of 19th Century Idealism* (New York: Farrar, Straus and Company, n.d.), p. 100.

17. Ruskin, *Unto This Last*, p. 39.

18. Ibid., p. 43.

19. Ibid., p. 79.

20. Ibid., pp. 56–57.

21. Ibid., p. 150.

22. John Ruskin, *Munera Pulveris* (New York: Longmans, Green, and Co., 1906), p. 152.

23. Ibid., p. 166.

24. In a later essay Arnold wrote: "Not that there is either any natural right in every man to the possession of a vote, or any gift of wisdom and virtue conferred by such possession. But if experience has established any one thing in this world, it has established this: that it is well for any great class and description of men in society to be able to say for itself what it wants, and not to have other classes, the so-called educated and intelligent classes, acting for it as its proctors, and supposed to understand its wants and to provide for them." How, one would like to know, did Ruskin react to these words? Matthew Arnold, "The Future of Liberalism," in *English Literature and Irish Politics*, ed. R. H. Super (Ann Arbor: University of Michigan Press, 1973), p. 140.

25. Matthew Arnold, "Democracy," in *The Portable Matthew Arnold*, ed. Lionel Trilling (New York: Viking Press, 1949), p. 441.

26. Ibid., pp. 442–43.

27. Ibid., p. 464.

28. Matthew Arnold, "Equality," in *The Portable Matthew Arnold*, p. 588.

29. Ibid., p. 600.

30. Matthew Arnold, "Friendship's Garland," in *Culture and Anarchy*, ed. R. H. Super (Ann Arbor: University of Michigan Press, 1965), p. 19.

31. Ibid., p. 331.

32. Ibid., p. 332.

33. Arnold, "The Future of Liberalism," p. 143.

34. Ibid., p. 144.

35. Ibid., p. 157.

36. Ibid., p. 159.

2

Two Worlds:
America's Search for High Culture

The German influence was profoundly felt in America as well as in England. From about 1840 onward the German writers began to appear in translation and set off a wave of anticapitalist idealism among students and intellectuals. "They all agreed regarding the state of the world," wrote Van Wyck Brooks. "It was a cold unfeeling civilization, bred by commercial interests and isolation."[1] Coleridge, Carlyle, and the Romantics also were avidly read in New England. Especially Carlyle. Much of the German influence reached America through him. Brooks says:

> Over the rising school of New England writers, even over the toughest-grained, Carlyle and Carlylese were to leave their traces. . . . He vindicated, they felt, their celestial birthright, showed them that the current ideals were shams, ridiculed the respectable . . . heroes of a mechanical age; he taught the "science of dynamics," the "primary, unmodified forces and energies of men, the mysterious springs of love and fear and wonder." He gave them faith in their own endeavors. He told them to quit their paper formulas and know that they were alive and that God was alive.[2]

Emerson and Thoreau: Loss of Self and the Making of Money

No one was more receptive to the gospel according to Carlyle than Emerson and the group of transcendentalists that had gathered about him. Emerson and Carlyle met on several occasions, and their correspondence fills two large volumes. Carlyle would one day say that Emerson was the only one "who completely understood" him. In the solitude of Concord, Emerson thought long and deep thoughts, read Plato and Goethe, and scanned the countryside around Walden Pond to discover the hidden handwriting of the gods. Eventually he found his voice and, in a style that sometimes sparkles like crossed swords, began to write against his age: against its avarice, its materialism, its preoccupation with bigness, its machines, and its money, and the leveling effects of democracy. To all of this he opposed the higher powers of nature, self-reliance, and the oversoul. Transcendentalism, said Emerson, is idealism. The world is divided into two realms: the unreal realm of appearances, sensations, and empirical science and the realm of ultimate reality, the unseen transcendental world where spirit has its abode. This realm can be discovered only through poetry and philosophy. Emerson's accent in this account is heavily Platonic, though we occasionally hear Hegel, as in the idea that God has reproduced himself in mind and nature. Culture is the struggle for the reunification of an original totality.

Emerson's philosophy provided a potent weapon against commerce and industry, though his criticism never reached the vitriolic heights of his English counterparts. This was perhaps because industrialism in America did not show the ugly face it did in England and because Emerson was inclined by his upbeat beliefs to see some dynamism and creative force in the industrial arts. In some of his earlier essays especially, he spoke favorably about the possibilities of technology, democracy, and commerce. He believed these to be not only congruent with but actually expressive of the moral core of transcendentalism. He said, for example, that trade was "the principle of liberty."[3] But even in an essay like "The Young American" where his enthusiasm for the industrial order and American democracy runs high, there is a sharp note of anticapitalism.

> I find no expression in our state papers or legislative debate, in our lyceums or churches, especially in our newspapers, of a high national feeling, no lofty counsels, that rightfully stir the blood. . . . They recommend conventional virtues, whatever will earn and preserve property; always the capitalist; the college, the church, the hospital, the theatre, the hotel, the road, the ship, of the capitalist,—whatever goes to secure, adorn, enlarge these, is good; what jeopardizes any of these is damnable.[4]

Emerson soon modifies his praise of trade by saying that "Trade was one instrument, but Trade is also but for a time, and must give way to somewhat broader and better, whose signs are already dawning in the sky."[5] What are these signs? "Beneficent socialism," the "communism" of France, Germany, and Switzerland, trade unions, repeal of the Corn Laws, and various experiences in communal living. The socialism of "The Young American" is topped off with an Arnoldian recommendation that "the highest end of government is the culture of men."[6]

Emerson's early enthusiasm for technology and commerce was eventually much toned down, indeed reversed. By the late 1840s, Leo Marx writes, "he had become more sceptical about the compatibility of the pastoral ideal and industrial progress. His second visit to England in 1847 was in many ways a turning point in his intellectual development and *English Traits* (1856) is one of our first and most penetrating studies of the new culture of industrialism."[7] Emerson is now coming over to the views of his English friend, Carlyle, in condemning technology, empiricism, and money. His essay on wealth is significant reading in this context. Emerson begins by observing that in no country is "so absolute a homage paid to wealth," and, more scathingly, "a natural fruit of England is the brutal political economy."[8] The "two disgraces" in England are to show disrespect to Church and state and to be poor. Emerson analyzes in some detail this drive of the English to wealth: in their productivity, in their technology, in their military might, in the alliance of wealth and politics, in the glorification of private property, in architecture and art, in mores and manners. He is not without admiration for what the English have accomplished; he praises the kernel of creativity beneath the materialism. "The English are so rich and seem to have established a tap-root in the bowels of the planet, because they are constitutionally fertile and creative."[9]

But Emerson the moralist is quick to pass judgment. There is great loss of culture and of self in all this making of money. He finds that "the machine unmans the user," the engineer is crushed, and trade is tyranny. "Dragon money with his paper wings" rules over all. Here is the moralist in full stride:

A man should not be a silk-worm, nor a nation a tent of caterpillars. The robust rural Saxon degenerates in the mills to the Leicester sockinger, to the imbecile Manchester spinner,—far on the way to be spiders and needles. The incessant repetition of the same handwork dwarfs the man, robs him of his strength, wit and versatility, to make a pin-polisher, a buckle-maker, or any other specialty; and presently, in a change of industry, whole towns are sacrificed like ant-hills, when the fashion of shoe-strings supersedes buckles, when cotton takes the place of linen, or railways of turnpikes, or when commons are inclosed by landlords.[10]

At present, Emerson concludes, England does not rule her wealth but is ruled by it; she is done in by her materialism; success fosters baseness. This social crisis requires the "deep cure" of simpler social organization and higher principles.

The spirit of capitalism contradicted the philosophical premise of Emerson's major essays. "Self-Reliance" is a case in point. There he wrote that a reliance on property and on material things is a sign of weakness. A cultivated man, he says, "becomes ashamed of his property, ashamed of what he has, out of a new sense of his being." This reasoning is faithful to the two-world principle of his idealism: what one has is accidental; what one is is essential. The former is subject to circumstance; the latter subject only to the laws of the mind. The contradiction is even better illustrated in that extraordinary essay "Experience." In fact, here the otherworldly tenor is so pronounced that all activities of this world pale to insignificance. Emerson has little taste for the mundane; no talent at all for the prosaic. Experience had always to be stretched to its poetic plenitude. In "Experience" Emerson sees reality as oblique, evanescent, and lubricious. Things slip and slide along the glittering surface of reality inevitably to dissolve in the thin mists of illusion. "An unnavigable sea washes with silent waves between us and the things we aim at and converse with."[11] What use in such a world to strive and struggle? Life is "a bubble and a scepticism, and a sleep within a sleep."[12] Young men die prematurely or "lose themselves in the crowd." In this flitting state, where reality is forever slipping through our fingers, there is but one constant: "Underneath the inharmonious and trivial particulars, is a musical perfection, the Ideal journeying always with us, the heaven without rent or seam. . . . The great and crescive self, rooted in absolute nature, supplants all relative existence, and ruins the kingdom of mortal friendship and love."[13] In this kingdom vulgarity (the vulgus) has no rights, no hopes, no possibilities.

Michael Moral offers this judicious analysis of Emerson:

> He could never reconcile himself to the values of a civilization which was essentially one of property, of fences, of exclusiveness. . . . Brilliantly critical of the emergent American commercialism, which necessarily seemed to involve cultural superficiality, Emerson was particularly virulent against the species of democracy that in fact often only demands conformity to depersonalizing custom, and a consequent sacrifice of individual autonomy, of self-reliance.[14]

Thoreau similarly struck a high transcendental note from the opening pages of *Walden*, his classic paean to the pastoral ideal. The tone is fastidious, high-minded, neurasthenic. Thoreau straightway identifies the cause of the modern malady with the market economy. Men are so occupied with "factitious cares and superfluously coarse labors," so enslaved to their tools and machines that the finest qualities of their natures are never realized.[15] The anticommercial spirit runs like a threnody throughout *Walden*. For example, Thoreau thinks the Irish could be better employed than by building the Fitchburg railroad (but does not seem sufficiently aware that the only real alternative facing most of them was starvation); he admires commerce for a certain enterprise and energy and lets his imagination roam as a freight train passes, but is determined "not to have my eyes put out and my ears spoiled by its smoke and steam and hissing"; he expresses great perturbation with modern institutions and inventions. Paradoxically, Thoreau combined his pastoralism with a shrewd Yankee business sense. He is Scroogelike in keeping his accounts, and one suspects he could have succeeded very well in business.

One admires Thoreau for many good reasons: his individualism in testing his powers against the raw forces of nature; his praise of simplicity, frugality, independence, and other fine virtues; his fortitude and ingenuity; and, above all, his ability, which is the sure mark of genius, to transform his idiosyncrasies into metaphor. Nonetheless, *Walden* is a profoundly misguided book, setting forth as it does a beguiling but spiritually deficient philosophy. Money, we are told, is not required "to buy one necessary of the soul." Still, money is required to buy the necessaries of the body, and the body, as Nietzsche tells us, is another way of talking about the soul. Idealism at the price of rigid dualisms is not impressive. Most men "lead lives of quiet desperation," Thoreau asserts. The assertion is scarcely self-evident; and even if it were true, Thoreau would have had no way of knowing it. He is effectively countered on this point by John Stuart Mill who, in response to the objection that happiness cannot be a rational goal of life because it is unattainable, defined happiness as "an existence made up of few and transitory pains, many and various pleasures" and pronounced such an existence "even now the lot of many."[16]

"I went to the woods," Thoreau informs us in words that have profoundly impressed generations of students, "because I wished to live deliberately, to front only the essential facts of life." But the essential facts of life are not to be found in the woods. Heidegger said human life is a *mitsein*, a being together. The philosopher John Macmurray says the moral act is the act that intends community. That may be going too far. Man does have, however, an undeniable social aspect that all philosophies must take into account. *Walden* as a moral ideal bypasses those human encounters—in the family, in the marketplace, in the community of our fellows—that make up the sinewy lineaments of life. Emerson said of his comrade: "If I knew only Thoreau, I should think cooperation of good men impossible."[17]

Precisely so. Thoreau's posture deliberately avoids the central human task of building a just and humane social order. It is therefore a cheap solution to the conflict of wills that is the driving force of history.

George Santayana: Becalmed in the Cultural Backwaters

Transcendentalism can be more fully understood against the long tradition of "genteelism," of which it is the logical culmination. It was George Santayana who first spoke of "the genteel tradition" in a lecture of that title at the University of California, Berkeley, in 1911. His essay "The Genteel Tradition in American Philosophy" bears study for the light it throws on the extent of anticapitalist sentiment in American society. America, Santayana argued, has been a country of two cultures. With regard to the higher things, traditional norms prevail; with regard to practical affairs, innovation rules. He stressed the disparity between these two mentalities:

> The truth is that one-half of the American mind, that not occupied intensely in practical affairs, has remained, I will not say high-and-dry, but slightly becalmed; it has floated gently in the backwater, while, alongside, in invention and industry and social organization the other half of the mind was leaping down a sort of Niagara Rapids. This division may be found symbolized in American architecture: a neat reproduction of the colonial mansion . . . stands beside the skyscraper. The American Will inhabits the skyscraper; the American Intellect inhabits the colonial mansion. The one is the sphere of the American man; the other, at least predominantly, of the American woman. The one is all aggressive enterprise; the other all genteel tradition.[18]

In his analysis of how the genteel tradition arose, Santayana notes its source in Calvinism, which he defines as the religion of "the agonized conscience." Calvinism asserts three things: "That sin exists, that sin is punished, and that it is a beautiful thing that sin should exist to be punished."[19] To be a Calvinist philosophically is to feel a "fierce pleasure in the existence of misery." In due course, the sense of sin abated in America; good will became the predominant virtue; and the nation developed remarkable skills in the material order.

According to Santayana the greatest American writers were Poe, Hawthorne, and Emerson. In some ways they went beyond the genteel tradition. Yet an abstract, bookish, "starved" quality characterized their writings—an inability to embrace experience wholly—that links them with what went before. They really had nothing to offer, says

Santayana, but a refined Calvinism—a less harsh, more self-indulgent, more catholic version of the old-time religion. Thus Emerson is a "cheery, childlike soul." This more positive attitude toward experience is generally reflected in the other component of the genteel tradition: transcendentalism. Transcendentalism, Santayana explains, "embodied in radical form, the spirit of Protestantism . . . it was autonomous, undismayed, calmly revolutionary."[20] It matched well the American temperament, for "it felt that Will was deeper than Intellect; it focused everything here and now, and asked all things to show their credentials at the bar of the young self, and to prove their value for this latest born moment."[21]

It is difficult for Americans to get beyond the genteel mentality. Santayana draws an analogy: just as Catholicism pervaded the minds of Renaissance scholars who might not have much believed in it, so in America there was "nothing articulate" to take the place of the genteel culture in either its Calvinistic or transcendental forms. Whitman was the only American writer to break the genteel bonds. Santayana does not find Whitman original, a good poet, or even an admirable person. But there is nothing of the genteel tradition reflected in his work. Santayana also cites William James as one who in significant ways transcends the tradition in which he was "tightly swaddled." What was important about James is that he broke down the dualistic rigidities of the genteel tradition by plunging mind and soul with riotous enthusiasm into the flux of experience and found it good, found it improvable, even found it intelligible. James, says Santayana, overcame the genteel tradition "in the romantic way by continuing it into its opposite . . . the genteel tradition was led a merry dance when it fell into the hands of a genuine and vigorous romanticist like William James."[22]

Santayana delivered "The Genteel Tradition in American Philosophy" just a few weeks before he was to leave America for the last time. He returned to the theme again and again, as a lonely adult will sometimes revisit a fondly remembered scene from childhood. In "Philosophical Opinion in America," delivered before the British Academy in 1918, and in "The Moral Background," published in 1921, he again discusses the philosophical influences that gave rise to the genteel tradition. These essays are as much disquisitions on the general nature and history of philosophy as an analysis of the genteel tradition. They are caustic, insightful, and uniformly elegant. Santayana appeared not to like the philosophical tradition of the West. He thought it too anthropocentric, too absorbed in artificial problems, too tied to its own history.

The main point he makes in these essays is that American philosophy is rooted in the genteel tradition. "It is either inspired by religious faith, and designed to defend it, or else it is created somewhat artificially in the larger universities, by deliberately posing problems which, without being very pressing to most Americans, are supposed to be necessary problems of thought."[23] American philosophy, by Santayana's account, is a direct offshoot of German idealism and bears a strong flavor of subjectivism and romanticism. A 1918 speech entitled "Materialism and Idealism" is a superb analysis of the American character. There is a touch of genius in this description:

> In his affections the American is seldom passionate, often deep, and always kindly. If it were given me to look into the depths of a man's heart, and I did not find goodwill at the bottom, I should say without any hesitation: you are not an American.

He then adds an important qualification:

> But as the American is an individualist his goodwill is not officious. His instinct is to think well of everybody, and to wish everybody well, but in a spirit of rough comradeship, expecting every man to stand on his own legs and to be helpful in his turn. When he has given his neighbor a chance he thinks he has done enough for him; but he feels it an absolute duty to do that. It will take some hammering to drive a coddling socialism into America.[24]

Michael Harrington take note!

These essays contain many interesting animadversions. Santayana notes, for example, that Americans are the most adventuresome, the most socially radical descendants of Europe, for they sailed the uncharted seas and tamed a continent. He observes that the great empty spaces of America generate freedom. (There is always in Santayana a close connection between geography and ideas.) He calls attention to the imaginative powers of Americans, their practicality, and their optimism toward the future. The American is "an idealist working on matter. Understanding as he does the material potentialities of things, he is successful in invention, conservative in reform, and quick in emergencies."[25] This is a keen and basically sacramental view of materialism: matter is pregnant with spiritual possibilities; it points beyond itself to ideal values and, like nature, prolixly issues in life and "breeds all sorts of warm passions and idle beauties." Money, says Santayana, has no value in itself for the American; it is the ready symbol of material grace, a concrete measure of "success, intelligence and power." Americans in general make, lose, and spend money "with a very light heart."[26]

24

This, however, may be more Santayana's view than that of the average American. He had that insouciance toward material goods which those who inherit their wealth can easily affect. Nonetheless he is on to an important point, rightly seeing that America is the least materialist of nations. Later, John Dewey stressed this same point. In his *Individualism Old and New* he wrote: "The American problem is that of making the material an active instrument in the creation of the life of ideas and art."[27] Like Santayana he was arguing against those who fail to see the spiritual depths in the American ethos. For both, ideal values not only must be congruent with their material base but must actually grow out of it. Still, while Santayana saw this clearly enough, his aristocratic bias prevented him from accepting it entirely. For all the brilliance of his analysis of the genteel tradition, Santayana remained congenitally a part of it. He did not believe in progress or democracy or commerce or any other modern value in the ascendancy during his lifetime. His elitist sensibility, unimaginably refined by a long career of contemplating the realms of being, prevented him from seeing what was humanly fulfilling in these emergent realities. These modern values, he remarks in a characteristically sniffish manner, should have increased leisure but have instead "increased the population, degraded labor, and diffused luxury." He did not like modern values precisely because they put "the genteel tradition at bay," to cite the title of another of his essays. Commerce was, in the final analysis, vulgar, which, from the aristocratic point of view, was the ultimate condemnation. What is most objectionable in Santayana is his insufferable attitude toward those who were improving their lot (both materially and spiritually, for the two always go together), but not in accordance with the lofty principles he personally advocated. Santayana's naturalism was a curious sort: it excluded so much that was natural. Bertrand Russell remembered aloofness and facile contempt as Santayana's chief defects. That judgment stands up well.

The Genteel Tradition: Disaffection with the Commercial Republic

In his excellent study of the genteel tradition, John Tomsich concentrates on these figures: Thomas Aldrich, Richard Gilder, Richard Stoddard, George Boker, Bayard Taylor, George Curtis, Charles Eliot Norton, and Edmund Stedman—

> a group of men who represented older values threatened by the rise of the city, who were Protestant in religion and English or North European in ancestry. The institutions they directed . . . constituted a formidable array of literary power

25

and status. There were the quality magazines—*Harper's Monthly, The Century, The Atlantic Monthly, The North American Review*—the major publishing firms, the major Eastern universities, the most influential social clubs, and the American Academy of Arts and Letters. To win recognition of this conglomerate, an author need only appear in the pages of *The Century*.[28]

This group virtually dictated the reading habits of the educated public and shaped the cultural life of the nineteenth century. Polls taken at the time placed them ahead of or equal in popularity to such writers (who enjoy better reputations today) as Henry James, Mark Twain, Henry Wadsworth Longfellow, James Russell Lowell, and John Greenleaf Whittier. Disaffection with commercialism was a constant theme in their writings, one that became more marked after the Civil War. Stoddard spoke of "cursed, cursed gold."[29] Boker reacted physically: "If there is anything that I loathe with my whole soul it is trade. The low, dirty, lying, swindling rascality that is practiced under the flag of trade not only affects me morally but makes me sick to my stomach."[30] Norton and Curtis were critics of laissez faire. These writers in a more or less common idiom criticized capitalism in the name of an anti-democratic, organic view of society that in general favored a central, paternalistic government. They were, says Tomsich, "fundamentally unsympathetic to the deepest forces of social change in American society—industrialization, urbanization, bureaucratization."[31]

Let us focus on Charles Eliot Norton's *Considerations on Some Recent Social Theories* as an expression of the genteel posture. Norton is upset by the chaos in society. He calls for "clear, vigorous and truthful thought" to set the times aright. His angle of criticism is basically conservative: He appeals to principles and to tradition and invariably opposes those European voices demanding "universal liberty, the establishment of Republics, and the direct government of the people by itself."[32]

Norton grants the seductive character of the revolutionary alarums. People everywhere, and often for good reason, are seduced by the promises of freedom. But, Norton cautions, love of liberty ought to be a principle rather than a passion. He criticizes the theories of Louis Kossuth, Giuseppe Mazzini, and Louis Blanc, whom he considers the leaders of the "republican cause" in Europe, because

> the fundamental principles of their political philosophy are such as would lead only to confusion, and would destroy the hope of progress; for their political system is founded upon the assumption that wisdom and power are derived directly and immediately from the people,—that is, from the great

mass of any nation; and, consequently, that political liberty is an inherent right of mankind, and that a republic is necessarily the best form of government.[33]

Norton is antisocialist to be sure; but, more to the point, he is antidemocratic. Kossuth's claim that "democracy is but the embodiment of freedom" is for Norton a foolish claim.[34] He considered an "offensive declamation" Mazzini's slogan: "God is God, and the people is his prophet."[35] Blanc's assertion that the people were sovereign was "extravagant."

Norton substitutes his own judgment of the people. He says:

> It is not, then, to this people that we are to look for wisdom and intelligence. It is not to them that we are to trust the progress of improvement. They could not, if they would, rescue themselves from evil; and they have no help for others. But their progress must be stimulated and guided by the few who have been blessed with the opportunities, and the rare genius, fitting them to lead. . . . It is the will of God—a will that we may not understand nor question—that progress should be very gradual; not visible from year to year, and only with difficulty to be seen from century to century.[36]

No divine could have put it better!

A false notion of the people, Norton thought, has its roots in a false doctrine of liberty, which holds it to be an inherent right of mankind. What is liberty? Norton asks. Certainly not a moral ideal. Norton restricts its meaning to "freedom from all restraints which may prevent the doing of what is right."[37] But freedom "from" is not sufficient; there must also be freedom "for." This "for" easily translates into the power to do the will of God. From there it is but one move to limit freedom by the authority of those who are appointed to do the interpreting. In Norton's theocratic view, this includes the government, for human law must reflect and harmonize with the law of God. There is not much freedom anywhere in the world, Norton observes. Moreover, it is in the nature of things that there not be. This does not mean that injustice is justified, but the fact of injustice is not an argument for universal liberty. Norton makes his point with some eloquence:

> Liberty is to be gained only by slow and arduous training. She is not to be seized by force; she is not to be compelled to unwilling service. Her presence may be decreed by ruler or by people, but she will not obey the decree. The efforts of men to gain Liberty, the struggles of the oppressed to

overthrow tyranny, the aspirations and the exertions everywhere for freedom, are to be cheered, encouraged, and aided. But encouragement and aid are not always to be given where the shout for freedom is the loudest.[38]

Because of his well delimited ideas of the people and of freedom, Norton does not think a universal republic—by which he means "the direct government of the people by itself"—is possible, let alone desirable. He gives two reasons for this. First, all right to govern is a delegated right; government is a question of expediency. No one form of government is intrinsically better than another (a remarkably antidemocratic claim in itself). "An absolute monarchy with piety is better for a people than a republic without it." Second, there is no direct connection between liberty and any form of government. "The spirit of liberty may grow in spite of bad government, or it may become extinct under a good one."[39] The same goes for tyranny. Thus Norton slowly edges the argument to the moral ground of education and culture. The degree of liberty as well as the vitality of government are functions of "general moral and intellectual education."[40] Although Norton believes that no form of government is inherently better than another, he concedes that in practice some are worse than others. A republican form of government would be the worst kind.

Norton's essay on socialism is, as one might expect, critical even though the ideal is praiseworthy. It is a sad fact that the earth is divided between those who lack the means to satisfy their spiritual and physical wants and those (a minority) who possess such means. We must constantly work to overcome this disparity, and, indeed, history does show that progress has been made over the ages and should continue. But socialism does not have the answer. Norton tries to prove that it rests "upon three mutually dependent errors,— those namely, of perfect equality among men, of the destruction of individual property, and of universal association. It has appeared, that, whether regarded in their moral, their political, or their economical relations, these ideas are equally erroneous."[41]

He clings to the belief that "no new system, no change in the economical relations of men, will alone bring about a better state of society."[42] He observes that some inequalities are natural and unalterable, arising from "the variety of God's dispensations to men."[43] Norton is thus able to shift the discussion to a religious plane. The kind of equality the social reformers want can only be accomplished by the power of religion; all human proposals to this end are doomed to frustration. Norton levels this argument against the socialist call for universal association: either people will enter into such association

28

voluntarily or they must be forced into it. The first is impossible and the second leads to tyranny. We cannot imagine, says Norton, that people would voluntarily enter into one great association. "This world does not offer a fair place for the trial of such a plan." Moreover, it supposes that "some of the ruling passions of mankind must be blotted out from it . . . the motives which have been in force since the beginning of the world must be changed."[44]

Norton comes down hard on Louis Blanc's prescription that under socialism everyone would give according to his abilities and receive according to his needs. The difficulty here, Norton notes, is that some authority would be required to legislate needs and abilities, someone to be the "judge of wants." A happy dream could easily degenerate into a relationship of masters and slaves. Such forced equality is, moreover, artificial and therefore inefficient; it ignores the natural rhythms of human relationships. Norton's judgment anticipates many later critiques of socialism:

> A fixed system of whatever sort that attempts to regulate all human relations, and to restrict the variety in human circumstances, which results from the differences in individuals, can only end in tyranny. Men are not placed in this world to sacrifice their individual characters and interests to the fancied advantage of other men.[45]

This sort of system had been tried as long ago as 600 B.C. in Sparta. It did not work then and, Norton believed, would not work in his time. Norton conducts a detailed review of the various experiments in association recently launched in Europe, particularly from 1848 onward. The vast majority of them either failed outright or were shortlived. They fed false expectations on the part of workers, encouraged "the hot sun of state favor," played into the hands of demagogues, and, overall, worked to the advantage of capital rather than labor. Norton acquits himself of an acute piece of social criticism in these pages and concludes his critique with this caustic pronouncement: "And in general, in regard to the associations, there was too much of this cant about brotherhood and equality,—a cant difficult to be borne with, since it tends to bring into disrepute the noblest principles, and to weaken their authority over the world."[46] Norton's philosophical base is straightforward utilitarianism. Society is a collection of individuals; the happiness of one promotes the happiness of others. "The progress of society is simply the progress of the individuals who compose it." The love of property, he asserts, "is the great and unvarying force in promoting the development of much of what is best in character."[47] And this judgment: "A system which would destroy individual property is a system which confounds the distinction between good and evil, would destroy an essential good for the purpose of getting rid of evils which have no necessary connection with it."[48]

We must not think that because Norton rejected socialism he accepted capitalism. Although he was less severe in his criticism of capitalism, he remained impressed by certain aspects of socialism. For example, he constantly approved of socialism as an ideal. More specifically, he held two progressive beliefs. First, he always believed in progress, not an extravagant or irresponsible progress but, nonetheless, a very real and inevitable progress that was scarcely compatible with his conservative principles. Second, he was truly moved by the plight of those suffering from inequality. He never seriously considered replacing capitalism, but he did mount a sustained criticism, partly inspired by his reading of socialist literature, against a system that he thought oppressive. He defends the right to property, but qualifies this right when he says that we have begun to learn

> the true tenure of such possessions, and to understand that no selfish claim to them is sufficient; that no *exclusive right* to them can be sustained; and that no title to earthly advantages, however ancient and hedged round it may be, is valid, unless it be supported by clearly acknowledged responsibilities and well-performed duties.[49]

And again: "It is not to be forgotten, that there is much unjust inequality to be remedied; that the abuses of property are what have chiefly led to the idea of its destruction; and that the free association of men in the pursuit of their own interests, under every different form, is one of the securities for progress."[50] He agrees with John Stuart Mill that workers should share in profits beyond their wages; he is respectful of efforts by the Christian Socialists, led by Frederick Maurice and Charles Kingsley, to reduce the gap between classes; and he favored labor unions. Norton also condemned slavery as an evil and refused to accept the conventional argument that it was a necessary evil.

It is easy to get the impression that Norton wants to have it both ways: to preserve the best in capitalism by cauterizing it with the best in socialism. But that would be an inaccurate impression. The truth is, Norton (and most of his compeers) criticized social and economic systems from the high ground of a body of moral principles. Measured against this canon all systems are found wanting, and often enough for the same reasons. Thus capitalism is condemned for appealing to materialism, wanton self-interest, irreligion. Norton is unequivocal about this.

> From the connection between the laws of morality and those which regulate the material concerns of men, it follows that the self-interest by which men are supposed to be urged in the pursuit of material satisfaction must be coincident. . . with that self-denial which is the requirement of morality, and which Christianity, above every other form of religion, establishes as the necessary discipline of virtue.[51]

Happiness is the legitimate goal of conduct; material wants must be satisfied as a step to this end, but "that self-interest is short-sighted and imperfect which does not see that the pursuit of material comfort is a folly, when disjoined from the practice of virtue."[52] Insofar as both capitalism and socialism concentrate on the satisfaction of material wants, they fail the moral test and will not lead to happiness, let alone Christian virtue. America is "the noblest field of progress."[53] Still, Norton is not sanguine about its future: "It may be the will of God that our own country should give another example of the insufficiency of material prosperity to preserve a people from decline."[54]

Norton's obsessive moralizing finally blurs his social commentary. He conflates the economic problem with religion on the one hand and with education on the other. He concludes his discussion of cooperative associations with the thought that only education will save the workers from their plight. "The first duty, the first necessity, is to help them to gain possession of their intellectual and moral natures. Till this is attained, liberty, fraternity, equality, association, are impossible."[55] Whether true or not, Norton is running too many things together here and fails to see, among other blindnesses, that the political economy is itself a powerful educational force. Because Norton was so bold a moral thinker, he was a timid social philosopher. This is another way of saying that much of his moral philosophy was alien to the social order he attempted to analyze. Tomsich puts it well:

> The modesty of Norton's proposals is typical. However strong were their theoretical objections to the doctrine of laissez-faire, the genteel group were exceedingly cautious in recommending any actual retreat from capitalism. They were suspicious of economic liberalism, but their suspicions were conservative. . . . In the end the genteel group seemed almost to revert to the individualism it had so long attacked. Unsuccessful in influencing the course of current politics and economics, the genteel writers turned to culture. There, for a time, they proved to be more potent.[56]

An interesting complement of Tomsich's study is Jackson Lears's *No Place for Grace: Antimodernism and the Transformation of American Culture 1880–1920.* Lears summons forth an extraordinary cast of characters. A biographical appendix lists the principals (sixty-seven in all), beginning with Brooks Adams and ending with Edith Wharton, and includes father's occupation, spouse, chief residences, chief occupations, education, and religious background and/or affiliation for each entry. These antimodernists were usually from well-educated, socially prominent families and, as the name suggests, rejected the modern values of democratic capitalism in favor of premodern values. More specifically, Lears finds five distinct tendencies among them. Some sought escape from modernity in arts and crafts ideology; another group sought escape in the martial ideal; a third group was attracted to the spiritual values of the Middle Ages; a fourth was attracted to modern forms of High Church (Catholic or Anglo-Catholic) liturgies; and significant numbers (including Charles Eliot Norton and Van Wyck Brooks) sought meaning in Oriental cultures.

The high point of Lears's book is an analysis of Henry Adams, the archetypical antimodernist. He passes this overall judgment:

> In America (as in Europe) antimodern sentiments affected more than a handful of intellectuals: they pervaded the middle and upper classes. Aesthetes and reformers sought to recover the hard but satisfying life of the medieval craftsman; militarists urged a rekindling of archaic martial vigor; doubters in religion yearned for the fierce convictions of the peasant and the ecstasies of the mystic.[57]

The antimodernists were not primarily from the political or economic sectors; they were overwhelmingly from the moral-cultural domain: writers, academics, religious leaders, journalists, and assorted intellectuals. They were existentialists before their time, protesting against the inauthentic conditions of modern life, seeking intense forms of experience and deeper meanings beyond those conditions.

Not far into Lears's book the reader realizes that he himself is the principal player in this stellar cast of antimodernists. In the preface Lears states: "I originally felt drawn to antimodernists because I shared their discontent with modern culture: its crackpot obsession with efficiency, its humanist hubris, its complacent creed of progress." He indicts capitalism for "its corrosive impact on family, craft, community, or faith" and follows with this intriguing blast: "in a society dedicated to economic development and personal growth at the expense of all larger loyalties, conservative values are too important to be left to pseudo-conservative apologists for capitalism." These apologists are not named, but the enemy is clearly identified. Lears's book has the dubious distinction of repeating virtually every charge ever leveled at democratic capitalism. By the time one reaches the epilogue, all Lears's cards are on the table. "Industrialism per se has played a major role in spreading the sense of unreality," and modern secular liberalism "has by now revealed the moral hollowness at its core."[58]

Lears attempts to strengthen his critique by adopting from the Italian Marxist Antonio Gramsci the concept of cultural hegemony. According to this theory, ruling social groups maintain their power not through force but by absorbing the opposition, by "winning the spontaneous loyalty of subordinate groups to a common set of values and attitudes."[59] Thus, paradoxically, the antimodernists served in the long run to strengthen capitalism. Lears traces the distant sources of our contemporary preoccupations with therapy, consumerism, and hedonism to the antimodernist movement. The arts and crafts movement degenerated into self-indulgence and thus foreshadowed the later culture of conspicuous consumption. The medievalists were the forerunners of the flower children of the 1960s. Lears puts it this way: "Antimodern longings for authentic experience, by promoting the self-absorption of the therapeutic world view, provided fertile emotional ground for the growth of the twentieth-century corporate system."[60] Regrettably, Lears does not argue strenuously for this view; rather it springs more or less full blown from his ideological perspective. Although interesting, this view is subject to the powerful counterargument that the features of contemporary social life Lears dwells on—the concerns with therapy, consumerism, hedonism, etc.— do not strengthen democratic capitalism. On the contrary, they weaken it. A powerful line of critics from Joseph Schumpeter to Daniel Bell has noted that democratic capitalism is being destroyed by its own success. Bell has persuasively argued that hedonism not only is foreign to capitalism, it threatens to tear it apart from within. Lears is a capable historian, but not a persuasive one.

The New Humanists: Protecting the Classical Heritage

The spirit of transcendentalism lived on in the antimodernists and, indeed, has had many reincarnations in American culture. Traces of it can be detected in the Social Gospel movement, in the Agrarian movement (and some of the schools of literary criticism that sprung from it), in neo-orthodoxy, in numerous educational reforms, in various socialisms, and most recently, in a somewhat degraded form, in the student unrest of the 1960s.[61] The most sustained effort to revive cultural idealism in the twentieth century was made by the New Humanists of the 1920s and early 1930s led by Irving Babbitt, professor of French at Harvard, Paul Elmer More, professor of philosophy and classics at Princeton (and editor of *The Nation* from 1909 to 1914), and Norman Foerster, professor of English at the University of Iowa. These Humanists drew their philosophical inspiration directly from Plato. The first Platonic postulate they embraced was an absolute dualism between man's higher and lower natures. Babbitt quotes Emerson in the epigraph of his *Literature and the American College:*

> There are two laws discrete
> Not reconciled, —
> Law for man, and law for thing;
> The last builds town and fleet,
> But it runs wild,
> And doth the man unking.[62]

Other classical beliefs adopted by the Humanists included the rule of moderation, the reality of the spiritual life, the identity of virtue and knowledge, and a hierarchical conception of reality (which implied some kind of aristocracy in politics).

The main concern of the New Humanists was to protect and promote the classical heritage. To this end they vigorously attacked the emerging naturalism (in science, philosophy, and literature), an attack that soon widened to a general critique of American society. The Humanists opposed educational reform (for in every educational reform the classics lost ground), humanitarianism in religion, romanticism in the arts (Rousseau was one of their favorite targets), liberalism in politics, and the growing democratic tenor of culture. Like their Victorian predecessors, they opposed, or at the very least were highly critical of, the modern trinity of democracy, science, and capitalism. On all sides they saw sentiment replacing judgment as the basis of cultural discrimination. One reason Rousseau drew so much fire was that they blamed him for externalizing the real dualism of man's nature into the false dualism of man against society. Society then becomes an easy scapegoat for individual responsibility, and human energies are dissipated in unproductive efforts to improve society when the chief task of ethics is self-improvement. The New Humanists were professed conservatives, indeed reactionaries. For what is reaction, asked More, but "to answer action with action," to measure the aimless flow of circumstances against steadfast norms, to bring the experience of the past to bear upon present experiences.

Matthew Arnold's influence on the New Humanists is strong because like him they were interested in the relationship between politics and culture—specifically, in the role of politics in promoting culture. They also admired Edmund Burke, as Arnold himself had.

They liked Burke's organic conception of the state as opposed to the atomistic and the individualistic theories of Hobbes or Rousseau. They did not want to believe that men were isolated units, but, of course, they did not want to be collectivists or determinists either. They appreciated individualism, but not to the extent of sacrificing a sense of history. Still, an inert traditionalism must be avoided. Burke helped the New Humanists find their bearing between these extremes.

The individualism they rejected derived not from the "utilitarian conception of life in general, but from the political economy of Adam Smith in particular. Let the State stand aside, says Adam Smith, and give the individual free swing (*laisser faire*). He will not abuse this freedom, for he will be guided by an enlightened self-interest."[63] Self-interest is all very well if it is understood as "profound thinkers" like Aristotle understood it. But, Babbitt states:

> the self that these thinkers have in mind is not the self that makes pursuit of wealth its first aim, but the ethical self that exercises control over this acquisitive self. Leave the acquisitive self without this control and the right kind of competition will degenerate into the wrong kind, the ruthless kind which was actually encouraged by the Manchester School of economics and in which mill operatives become mere "cannon-fodder" in the industrial warfare.[64]

Babbitt makes a similar distinction about property. "One may, indeed, lay down the principle that, if property as a means to an end is the necessary basis of civilization, property as an end itself is materialism."[65] Under no circumstances is priority to be given to material goods. Given the "insatiableness" of human nature, our desires must be disciplined. Babbitt, quoting Aristotle, says that the only remedy for economic equality is to educate nobler types not to desire more; it is desires, not possessions, that must be equalized.

The New Humanists argue for discrimination also toward democracy. "If democracy means simply the attempt to eliminate the qualitative and selective principle in favor of some general will, based in turn on a theory of natural rights, it may prove to be only a form of the vertigo of the abyss."[66] This, they said, is what they perceived to have happened in their time. Democracy legitimizes a mad scramble for money and material success; the multimillionaire has become the representative product of a country dedicated to equality.

One of Babbitt's students at Harvard was T. S. Eliot. Some of his influence is apparent in Eliot's *The Idea of a Christian Society*. Eliot says, for example: "The more highly industrialized the country, the more easily a materialistic philosophy will flourish in it and the more deadly that philosophy will be. . . . The tendency of unlimited industrialism is to create bodies of men and women detached from tradition, alienated from religion and susceptible to mass suggestion; in other words, a mob."[67] Capitalism is antithetical to Christian society, Eliot stated, because it favors the profit motive, exploits the worker and natural resources, and accords unfair advantage to the rich.

Babbitt is unsparing in his judgment of the commercial man. The following quotations are characteristic of his criticism: "For one may affirm with some confidence that a man who thinks it worthwhile to pile up an income said to be greater than that of J. D. Rockefeller is not engaged in a very energetic humanist or religious working."[68] "To a person with a proportionate view of life it might seem rather to be full blown commercial insolence."[69] "Commercialism is laying great greasy paws upon everything; so that, whatever democracy may be theoretically, one is sometimes tempted to define it practically as standardized and commercial melodrama."[70] "The American reading his Sunday paper in a state of lazy collapse is perhaps the most perfect symbol of the triumph of quantity over quality that the world has yet seen."[71] "We are in danger of producing in the name of democracy one of the most trifling brands of the human species the world has yet seen."[72]

Paul Elmer More's position is not substantially different. He defended dualism, which he imbibed directly from Plato, as an elementary datum of experience.[73] We encounter dualism, he said, each time we raise the question of our better self. He favored a natural aristocracy based on an intimate connection between imagination and leadership. Artists, the custodians of the imagination, ought to form a close alliance with "natural" leaders. His principal objection to democracy was that it tended to reject its best leaders. More detested Theodore Roosevelt, seeing in him the very embodiment of demagoguery and sentimentality. The difficult question he takes up in the essays published as *Aristocracy and Justice* is how a conservative notion of leadership can be effectively wedded with popular demands. The closest he comes to an answer is to redefine the problem of leadership as a problem of education and to recommend the classics as the best course of study for forming a natural aristocracy.

More also defended property. He said often that "the rights of property are more important than the right to life."[74] But he did not defend capitalism. He was highly critical of "the Gospel of wealth." He thought moguls like Charles Schwab, John D. Rockefeller, and Andrew Carnegie had a bad effect on public morals. In 1902 he published an essay entitled "Wealth and Culture" in which he described Wall Street as "the most genuine expression of our national life."[75] The buildings there stand to American culture as the Parthenon to Athens, the Louvre to Paris, or St. Peter's to Rome. By contrast, "churches, colleges and museums dwindle in impressiveness to mere toys."[76] Wall Street is the symbol of all that is original, creative, and ideal in the American spirit, the end toward which the history of the human race has been obscurely tending.

For all of that, Wall Street is not a respectable cultural ideal. It produces a degraded literature. No literature "of permanent greatness or loveliness" can be inspired by such an ideal.[77] It is naught but materialism that imprisons the mind and leads to pathos and cynicism. Wealth crushes those whom it blesses. A change must come from "some new and fairer vision of life to supplant this present ideal of wealth which has been fostered into such predominance by the sudden and enormous increase in the mechanical facilities for producing wealth."[78] A constant theme in More's social criticism is that wealth generates an ethics of sympathy (found in both Adam Smith and Rousseau), which tends to run rampant in democratic societies as humanitarianism and socialism.

As an inveterate book reviewer, More encountered the ethics of sympathy often in Social Gospel novels, in realist fiction on social and economic problems, and in radical novels like Upton Sinclair's *The Jungle* and Jack London's *The Iron Heel*. He seldom reviewed such books because they revealed a proletariat cowering in fear and antagonism while the upper classes resort to humanitarian sops. Much better, says More, is the traditional fear of God to motivate authentic morality. He did review at some length Florence Converse's *The Burden of Christopher*, a representative expression of what he called the "new morality." The novel deals with an idealistic young man who conducts business on a profit-sharing basis "for the benefit of the community." More uses the occasion to get some digs in at starry-eyed academic economists, but principally to oppose to this morality his own tougher brand, which "is not determined essentially by the relation of a man to his fellows or by their approval, but by the consciousness of rightness in the man's own breast."[79] Obligation to society is neither the primal law nor the source of integrity; social justice is subordinate to individual character; equality or opportunity takes second place to a sense of duty.

It is clear, says David Hoeveler, in a fair judgment of the New Humanists, that they

> shared many social views with the earlier Victorian critics of democracy, especially Carlyle, Ruskin and Arnold. . . . They upheld an organic view of society against an atomistic and

individualistic one and were also severely adverse to traditional laissez-faire economics. With Ruskin they condemned economic orthodoxy for its one sided view of human nature and saw its endorsement of the acquisitive and competitive instincts playing directly into the hands of the Nietzschean individualists. The ethics of power built on this tradition had so brutalized American life that it elicited even from More a note of compassion: "History pronounces the philosophy of Manchester one of the most heartless creations of the human brain." The New Humanists had no faith in the masses, turned with distaste from the values and quality of mass society, and tolerated no leveling schemes of social reform.[80]

The Humanist movement peaked in 1930 with the appearance of Norman Foerster's *Humanism in America*, a collection of essays by members of the group. The debate was joined almost immediately by the publication of *The Critique of Humanism*, which included articles by such well-known critics as Allen Tate, R. P. Blackmur, Edmund Wilson, Malcolm Cowley, Kenneth Burke, and Lewis Mumford. There is no doubt that the New Humanists got the worst of it. Blackmur, for example, charged that they did not understand American society and therefore measured it by foreign standards. Malcolm Cowley put it more bluntly: the New Humanism, he said, "is only a collection of conservative, snobbish, theological, and puritanical attitudes and beliefs which can never humanize society."[81]

The Agrarians: Thunder in the Old South

This overview may profitably be rounded out with a brief consideration of the influential movement in American culture known as Agrarianism. The Agrarians were first known as "the Fugitive Group" (after a magazine they published) who gathered under the leadership of John Crowe Ransom at Vanderbilt University during World War I. Their interests initially were purely literary, but in time expanded to politics and economics. Agrarianism developed independently of the New Humanism, but the two movements shared a common posture: both were dualistic, conservative, and proreligious. In addition, the Agrarians saw the locus of their values in the South rather than in the North, in the country rather than in the city.

There were three major statements of Agrarian philosophy. The first was an essay by Ransom published in *The Sewanee Review*, April 1928, entitled "The South—Old or New." He argued that the superiority of the South rests on two facts: the European principles that pervade its culture and its antimaterialism. In the South industrial concerns were happily subordinate to "a leisure which permitted the maximum activity of intelligence." Since the victory of the North in the Civil War and the triumph of industrialism, the urgent question had become, as Ransom interpreted events: "How can the Southern communities, the chief instance of the stationary European principle of culture in America, be reinforced in their ancient integrity as centers of resistance to an all-but-devouring industrialism?" There is no doubt that Ransom romanticized the possibilities for the good life in the South (most of which existed in wretched poverty) as much as he exaggerated the stability of European principles.

Still, his essay was the first salvo of what was to become a full-fledged manifesto by twelve Southerners published in 1930 as *I'll Take My Stand*, the second major statement of Agrarian philosophy. The thesis of these essays is that industrialism would be the ruin of the South. The gentleman farmer was held forth as the model of the good life. To the modernist trinity of values (democracy, capitalism, and science) the contributors to *I'll Take My Stand* opposed nature, art, and religion. Their animus against business, univocally associated with an insatiable lust for material accumulation, is unrelenting. The simplistic dualism of North and South provided an appropriate conveyor for the most cherished ideas of the Agrarians. As John L. Steward described the Agrarian's dualism: "The North—bleak, abstract, materialistic, greedy, arrogant—is the realm of reason. The South—florid, concrete, interested in little charming things of no utility, gentle and inclined to give way rather than quarrel shrilly—is the realm of sensibility." And he adds: "For all the elegance and persuasiveness of the prose style, this was bad history, worse geography, and completely impossible psychology."[82]

This quotation from the book's "Statement of Principles" (written by Ransom) states clearly the Agrarian case against capitalism:

> Religion can hardly expect to flourish in an industrial society. Religion is our submission to the general intention of a nature that is fairly inscrutable; it is the sense of our role as creatures within it. But nature industrialized, transformed into cities and artificial habitations, manufactured into commodities, is no longer nature but a highly simplified picture of nature. We receive the illusion of having power over nature, and lose the sense of nature as something mysterious and contingent. The God of nature under these conditions is merely an amiable expression a superfluity, and the philosophical understanding ordinarily carried in the religious experience is not there for us to have.

Nor do the arts have a proper life under industrialism, with the general decay of sensibility which attends it. Art depends, in general, like religion, on a right attitude to nature; and in particular on a free and disinterested observation of nature that occurs only in leisure. Neither the creation nor the understanding of works of art is possible in an industrial age except by some local and unlikely suspension of the industrial drive.

The amenities of life also suffer under the curse of a strictly business or industrial civilization. They consist in such practices as manners, conversation, hospitality, sympathy, family life, romantic love—in the social exchanges which reveal and develop sensibility in human affairs. If religion and the arts are founded on right relations of man-to-nature, these are founded on right relations of man-to-man.[83]

These views are expanded in the third major statement of Agrarian philosophy, Ransom's own book *God Without Thunder* (also published in 1930). The root of our problem, he argues here, is our substitution of science for religion. As a consequence industrialism "governs our whole manner of life," and it is, Ransom adds, "a miserable fate for any people to suffer."[84] Moreover, "under industrialism, which we conceive to be our divinely appointed mission, we scourge ourselves like true fanatics."[85] This is how he fancies the meaning of human life according to industrialism:

Industrialism assumes that man is merely a creature of instincts. That is, he is essentially an animal with native appetites that he must satisfy at the expense of his environment. His life consists entirely in the satisfaction of his appetites. But he differs from the other animals in one glorious particular: he has a reason. And what is its function? His reason is a superior cunning that enables him to get the objects of appetite out of nature faster, in greater purity, and in more abundance than they can. His reason is his science, and its characteristic act is to supply him with a process or with a tool which will wrest from nature with ridiculous ease the objects of his desire. In other words, man is an animal, but with a reason which permits him to live a life more animal than that of animals. For his reason serves his instinct, and concentrates and brutalizes the usual process of desire and satisfaction.[86]

God Without Thunder expands on the themes adumbrated in the author's "Statement of Principles," especially the theme of leisure. He evokes a rather farfetched picture of primitive society in which little time is spent procuring food and much in enjoying it. Primitive folk, we are told, "prolong the moment of satisfaction, and develop a rite of eating, a decorum, a studied leisure, and an art."[87] Science and industry, however, destroy enjoyment by speeding everything up. They "divest labor of its dignity and make it servile. So they have set up the modern industrial system: a system which may be defined outwardly as producing goods as fast as possible, and inwardly as deliberately sacrificing the enjoyment of labor."[88] Ransom embraces once again the Agrarian theme: agriculture is the privileged form of labor; routine and servile labor are foreign to farming; farmers work "inevitably at a leisurely gait"; farming is "infinite" in its variety and, unbelievably, "there was no curse" on farm labor.[89] For one promoting rigorous orthodoxy in religion and attempting "to restore to God the thunder," this is a curious reading of Scripture. Quite clearly Ransom is confusing fact and fiction!

Ransom reexamines the distinction between reason and sensibility in *God Without Thunder* and speaks of culture as "having and defending a delicate sensibility even while we are engaged upon the stern drive of the practical life."[90] As lovers betray their sensibility to become roués, so industrialists betray it in becoming producers. The God of olden days was inscrutable, but man could live comfortably in His world; the new God of Science "conferred upon man the grievous responsibility of being God-like in the sense of practicing evolution or practicing acceleration. And such doctrines as these are the causes and the aggravations of our present distress."[91]

Modernism: A Kingdom Jealously Guarded

The New Criticism, which Ransom and other Agrarians did so much to foster, became an important building block of Modernism in art and literature. Modernism was in fundamental ways antimodern. Many of the central poems, great novels, and art masterpieces of the Modernist movement were tightly wrapped in the values of a small but talented and influential body of writers who had a vested interest in denigrating modern experience. Their kingdom has been jealously guarded by a cultural establishment of English professors, art critics, museum directors, and other votaries of that establishment.

In his 1960 essay entitled "In Defense of Ignorance," the poet Karl Shapiro berated his peers for their hostility to modern life. He called them cultural Bolshevists and wrote that "in poetry it has been a fad, since Eliot, to condemn every aspect of contemporary life. . . . Modern poetry is a dangerous psychological evil, reinforcing every form of split between man and his world."[92] Modernist writers invariably see modern life as alienated, broken, soul-destroying. Shapiro's analysis points to the conclusion that Modernism, in its highest manifestations, is divorced from popular culture, from the activities of ordinary people, and from the unifying rhythms of nature. Full of lamentations and a critical concern for its own inner dynamics, such art fails to unify, to clarify, or to praise our experience.

For some years I taught a course entitled The Modern Temper. I gave it up recently because all the core texts painted life in such bleak tones, as a problem to which there could be only apocalyptic solutions. I remember quite distinctly the occasion of my decision not to continue with the course. After a term with Saul Bellow's *Herzog,* André Gide's *The Immoralist,* and T. S. Eliot's *The Wasteland* (all of which quite vividly portray the collapse of moral personality), Flannery O'Connor's *The Violent Bear It Away* and Graham Greene's *The Power and the Glory* (two excursions into darker reaches of faith), and André Malraux's *Man's Fate* (advocating revolution as the solution to the pain of modern existence), we came finally to consider Robinson Jeffers's *The Double Axe.* The bleak stoicism of that long work made me realize that there was something basically unjust about force-feeding students with a literature that denies practically everything their instincts and experience affirm. Students instinctively reject Modernism and are able to resist in large numbers and for long periods of time the efforts of professors to convert them to the higher culture. Most students, as an understandable defense, study economics and engineering instead. To be sick is to be human, said Jeffers, and he prays God to exterminate the race of men. In Jeffers, as in so much modern literature, humanism becomes inhumanism. Saul Bellow recently complained that writers cannot get into the minds of people absorbed in the works of a commercial republic. Why not? is the interesting question to be asked here. I would not deny that there is benefit to be derived from modern literature; it has in its way extended the range of human creativity. But I take my stand with Lionel Trilling who criticized a "radically anti-cultural" bias as the most important attribute of the modern imagination.

Modernism also finds expression in an important strand of social criticism. Shapiro is profoundly insightful when he observes that much social science today is a substitute for poetry. As late as the mid-nineteenth century what we now call the social sciences were part of the humanities, and particularly a part of moral philosophy. It is not surprising, therefore, that they too have become a vehicle of criticism of modern life similar to that of the high culture. This criticism becomes especially acute when it is flavored by Marxism, as in the Frankfort school. In America Herbert Marcuse expresses perhaps the most familiar version of the Frankfort thesis. In modern industrial societies, that thesis goes, our social lives are unfree, one dimensional, and indeed totalitarian. Marcuse does not shy from so strong a word. Capitalism, abetted by technology, has expanded to fill all our social space; it has become a political as well as a psychological universe. This totalitarian power maintains its hegemony by depriving all opposition of its critical function, that is, its capacity to think negatively against the system, and by imposing false needs through advertising, market control, and the media. Liberty itself thus becomes an instrument of domination, and reason conceals the dark side of irrationality. As a consequence all of our legitimating beliefs are rooted in "false consciousness."

The Frankfort solution to this predicament is to elaborate a critical theory intended to free us from false consciousness and restore our creative powers as rational beings. Jürgen Habermas, another well-known member of the Frankfort school, conceives of an ideal speech situation in which our reason is uncontaminated by any falsifying conditions. Rationality could have its way, and through untrammeled discussion we could demystify the prevailing power structure of society, see through its unfreedom, its inequality, and its coercion. It helps, I think, to see the claim that we become emancipated through critical theory as an updated version of the Socratic axiom that virtue is knowledge. Socrates set about dispelling the mysterious utterances of the Delphic oracle through dialectic, a method of testing opinions through rigorous questioning in order to refute them as untenable or to confirm them on the basis of reasons made self-conscious. Dialectic leads Socrates to a truer self, a novel (in his time) conception of the psyche as a capacity for intellectual judgment and enlightened moral action. Human excellence is the outcome of rationally perfected habits of talking, debating, and arguing. Quite naturally, a state composed of such enlightened individuals would be a free state, an ideologically pure state.

That this ideal did not come to pass in Socrates' day takes nothing away from its attractiveness. The Frankfortian ideal is similarly compelling. Who would not want a truer consciousness and a freer, multidimensional life? But this does not seem to be an easy matter. So we must press on to ask what is false about the Frankfortian effort to dispel false consciousness in all of its guises. One could say in a general way that it is an impossibly utopian effort, that human nature being what it is we cannot hope to exorcize all the unconscious influences that bear upon the ways we think and act and build our societies. How many layers of experience would have to be peeled away before we reach that mythic core of our true selves, our real interests? I will suggest, in addition, two more specific criticisms to this Frankfortian ideal.

First, there is something strange and unnatural about postulating a false consciousness as the initial datum. It is much better, Sartre advised us, to see the world as though it had its source in human freedom. So too the social world. Despite the limitations of ignorance and the human proclivity to self-deception, the postulate of freedom is defensible. If freedom is the fundamental human reality, then we cannot all be hoodwinked by oppressive social institutions, for these institutions represent choices, our choices. Freedom is never unlimited or ideologically pure; it is expressed in choices that are to be found in traditions, in habits and customs, in the multiple ways people cope with existence and define themselves through their daily activities. To reverse a famous (but false) axiom, we may say that man is born in chains but is everywhere free. The Frankfort criticism is as much indebted to Descartes as to Marx, for Descartes envisaged a world in which an evil demon was bent upon the deception of all mortals. Descartes too sought refuge from deception in a hyper-rationality, a haven of clear and distinct ideas where he was secure from the blandishments of the deceiving demon. But in fact there is no such haven. We create our meanings and bear the burden of freedom always in partial darkness.

A second criticism is the question of who will lead us from the oppression of false consciousness to the promised land of critical enlightenment. Under whose auspices will the therapeutic journey be conducted? Who is qualified to tell me that my true self is something other than what I think it is, or my true interests lie elsewhere than where I think I find them? It is true that I may be deceived. But then so might my liberators. Their claim to a superior way may be nothing more than the arrogance of rationalism.

In a discussion of Jürgen Habermas in the October 7, 1982, *New York Review of Books,* Quentin Skinner draws an illuminating analogy. Reading Habermas, he says, is like reading Martin Luther. Both call upon us to reform our sinful ways; both place high estimate on the rational properties of the Word. What confronts us in Habermas, says Skinner, is a variation on the ancient dialectic of sin and salvation. Although inspiring, this dialectic does not necessarily advance the cause of social philosophy.

Social criticism of the type under review reinforces the claims of the New Class, a new knowledge elite. What makes this class new is its skill in translating knowledge into social power. It therefore has a high stake in controlling the ways in which that knowledge is produced and socially implemented. Knowledge is always power, as

Francis Bacon rightly perceived. Today the power of the knowledge elite is vastly enhanced by advances in communications technology and by the expanded role of public agencies. Its promise to demystify is tantamount to a bid for political power.

The cultural curve from Emerson to contemporary social criticism is continuous and central. It defined the mainstream "humanistic" mentality and constituted an essential component of the American experience. That this is still so largely the case means we have not yet climbed out of the genteel tradition, not altogether. We are still a country of two cultures, one of higher things and one of practical affairs. High culture is commandeered by an intellectual elite; commerce is regarded as of a lower order, an intruder in culture's house of sweetness and light. This narrow notion of humanism creates in America the special problem of cutting off large areas of experience from a humanizing influence. In this sense our humanists have let us down badly. But the joke may be on them. It may be that there is more humanism in the commercial order they decry than in the high culture with which they identify.

Notes

1. Van Wyck Brooks, *The Flowering of New England 1815–1865* (New York: World Publishing Company, 1936), p. 181.

2. Ibid., p. 194.

3. Ralph Waldo Emerson, "The Young American," in *Nature, Addresses, and Lectures* (Boston, Mass.: Houghton Mifflin, 1855), p. 366.

4. Ibid., p. 234.

5. Ibid., p. 358.

6. Ibid., p. 235.

7. Leo Marx, *The Machine in the Garden* (New York: Oxford University Press, 1964), p. 263.

8. Ralph Waldo Emerson, *English Traits*, ed. Howard Mumford Jones (Cambridge, Mass.: Harvard University Press, 1966), pp. 99,100.

9. Ibid., p. 107.

10. Ibid., p. 108.

11. Ralph Waldo Emerson, "Experience," in *Selected Writings of Ralph Waldo Emerson*, ed. William H. Gilman (New York: New American Library, 1965), p. 329.

12. Ibid.

13. Ibid., p. 243.

14. Michael Moral, "Emerson," in *The Encyclopedia of Philosophy*, vol. 2, ed. Paul Edwards (New York: Macmillan, 1967), p. 479.

15. All quotations from *Walden* are from the Amsco School Publications edition (New York, n.d.).

16. John Stuart Mill, *Utilitarianism,* ed. Oskar Piest (Indianapolis, Ind.: Bobbs-Merrill, 1957), p. 17.

17. Quoted by Richard Poirier in a review of *Emerson in His Journals, New York Times Book Review,* June 20, 1982, p. 20.

18. George Santayana, *The Genteel Tradition,* ed. Douglas Wilson (Cambridge, Mass.: Harvard University Press, 1967), pp. 39–40.

19. Ibid., p. 41.

20. Ibid., p. 47.

21. Ibid., p. 53.

22. Ibid., p. 54. This is an interesting interpretation. Santayana may be right, though I have always found in James a driving Puritanism, the agonized conscience and brooding sense of evil of his forebears lingering beneath his high-spiritedness and buoyancy. His empiricism, however, is genuine enough. Indeed James himself thought of it as "radical," though that is not all there is to him.

23. Ibid., p. 102.

24. Ibid., p. 122.

25. Ibid., p. 124.

26. Ibid., p. 127.

27. John Dewey, *Individualism Old and New* (New York: Capricon, 1930), p. 126.

28. John Tomsich, *A Genteel Endeavor: American Culture and Politics in the Gilded Age* (Stanford, Calif.: Stanford University Press, 1971), p. 5.

29. Ibid., p. 139.

30. Ibid., pp. 139–40.

31. Ibid., p. 187.

32. Charles Eliot Norton, *Considerations on Some Recent Social Theories* (Boston, Mass.: Little, Brown, and Co., 1853), p. 3.

33. Ibid., pp. 6–7.

34. Ibid., p. 8.

35. Ibid., p. 9.

36. Ibid., pp. 19–20.

37. Ibid., p. 26.

38. Ibid., p. 35.

39. Ibid., p. 43.

40. Ibid., p. 44.

41. Ibid., p. 79.

42. Ibid., p. 56.

43. Ibid., p. 60.

44. Ibid., p. 66.

45. Ibid., pp. 72–74.

46. Ibid., p. 105.

47. Ibid., p. 75.

48. Ibid., p. 72.

49. Ibid., p. 55. Emphasis added.

50. Ibid., p. 80.

51. Ibid., p. 143.

52. Ibid., p. 144.

53. Ibid., p. 130.

54. Ibid., p. 157.

55. Ibid., p. 119.

56. Tomsich, *A Genteel Endeavor*, pp. 100–112.

57. Jackson Lears, *No Place of Grace: Antimodernism and the Transformation of American Culture 1880–1920* (New York: Pantheon Books, 1981), p. xiii.

58. Ibid., pp. 304, 307.

59. Ibid., p. xv.

60. Ibid., p. 303.

61. In his *The Higher Learning in America* (New Haven, Conn.: Yale University Press, 1936), Robert Hutchins cites as the first cause of confusion in higher education the love of money. "It is sad but true," he writes, "that when an institution determines to do something in order to get money it must lose its soul, and frequently does not get the money" (p. 4).

62. Irving Babbitt, *Literature and the American College* (Boston, Mass.: Houghton Mifflin, 1908).

63. Irving Babbitt, *Democracy and Leadership* (Boston, Mass.: Houghton Mifflin, 1924), p. 213.

64. Ibid., p. 214.

65. Ibid., pp. 203–4.

66. Ibid., p. 245.

67. T. S. Eliot, *The Idea of a Christian Society* (London: Faber and Faber, 1939), p. 21.

68. Ibid., p. 212.

69. Ibid., p. 239.

70. Ibid., p. 242.

71. Ibid., p. 243.

72. Ibid.

73. He also learned much about dualism from Emerson. Professor Duggan makes this observation: "Plato, he admitted, had 'perhaps alone of the philosophers' reconciled the Greek notion of the infinite with the Oriental notion of impersonality; but Emerson made this Platonic discovery 'the kernel of his doctrine.'" More concluded in 1894, "that anyone who understood the meaning of dualism as Emerson proposed it in *Fate* had no need to study Sanskrit for the wisdom of the East." See Francis X. Duggan, *Paul Elmer More* (New York: Twayne Publishers, 1966), p. 29.

74. T. S. Eliot, *The Idea of a Christian Society*, p. 21.

75. Paul Elmer More, "Wealth and Culture," in *The Essential Paul Elmer More*, ed. Byron C. Lambert (New Rochelle, N.Y.: Arlington House, 1972), pp. 342–58.

76. Ibid., p. 346.

77. Ibid., p. 348.

78. Ibid., p. 349.

79. Paul Elmer More, "The New Morality," in *The Essential Paul Elmer More*, p. 339.

80. J. David Hoeveler, Jr., *The New Humanism: A Critique of Modern America, 1900–1940* (Charlottesville: University Press of Virginia, 1977), pp. 137–38.

81. C. Hartley Grattan, ed., *The Critique of Humanism: A Symposium* (New York: Brewer and Warren, 1930), p. 92.

82. John L. Steward, *The Burden of Time: The Fugitives and Agrarians* (Princeton, N.J.: Princeton University Press, 1965), p. 151.

83. Ibid., pp. 151–52.

84. Ibid., p. 186.

85. Ibid., p. 188.

86. John Crowe Ransom, *God Without Thunder: An Unorthodox Defense of Orthodoxy* (Hamden, Conn.: Archon Books, 1965), p. 185.

87. Ibid., p. 192.

88. Ibid., p. 193.

89. Ibid., p. 195.

90. Ibid., p. 198.

91. Ibid., p. 205.

92. Karl Shapiro, "What Is Not Poetry," in *The Poet's Work*, ed. Reginald Gibbons (Boston, Mass.: Houghton Mifflin, 1979), pp. 104, 108.

3

Democratic Capitalism:
The Other Humanism

The critics of capitalism amply demonstrate the hazards of coming to social problems with ethical and philosophical conceptions preformed in the mold of idealism. Such conceptions risk being little more than prejudices, doomed to be ineffectual. Thus it comes as no surprise that these critics had little effect on the broad political and economic tendencies of their day. They succeeded rather well, however, in keeping an antimodern animus alive among humanists of a certain stripe.

Ernest Barker has shrewdly observed that humanists tend to be Platonists in social matters.[1] That is both a strength and a weakness. It is a strength because idealism is a powerful philosophy when supported, as in the works of Plato, by compelling metaphors. It is a weakness because the characteristic fallacy of idealism is its inability to make creative contact with the concrete world. The malady of idealism, notably in its Romantic expressions, is, as Nietzsche diagnosed it, "a severance of mind from world, soul from circumstance, human inwardness from external conditions."[2] Whence the most representative quality of modern man is "the strange contrast between an inner life to which nothing outward corresponds, and an outward existence unrelated to what is within."[3]

My discussion appears to lead toward the conclusion that idealism is no fit philosophy for this world. That is not quite my point. Rather, idealism in the hands of the critics reviewed was less an instrument of inquiry than a bludgeon. That is a pity, for the world is always in need of the moral vision idealism can supply. This is especially true of our world, ravaged as it is by boredom and foundering for want of directive ideals.

The critics of capitalism failed to grasp the dialectical relationship between the ideal and the real that characterize an integral humanism. Further, they did not understand that ideal fulfillment cannot be imposed from above, but must grow out of the nature of the materials. Because they feared contact with the world of modern values, they defined themselves negatively to that world. It is unfortunate that the critics of capitalism did not make better use of their sources, that they did not bring these to bear upon the problems of society more persuasively than they did. They missed a golden opportunity, and we are all the poorer for it. In abler hands, idealism could have mediated between the realities of the world and the demands of the spirit.

This important work of integration remains to be done. Neither the socialists nor the custodians of high culture have succeeded in giving democratic capitalism a reasoned place within their humanistic framework. Yet democratic capitalism is itself a humanism. When the critics of both the left and the right come to understand this, an important new chapter of social discourse will begin. Just why they have not yet understood it is a complicated question. Part of the problem is the way humanism has come to be defined in our culture. The Renaissance humanists, who contributed so heavily to this definition, were deficient humanists in precisely the same way their modern counterparts are deficient. The Renaissance humanists, after all, discovered not modern but ancient values; they lauded the superiority of the classical tradition; their values were the values of a premodern culture assumed to have primacy. This cannot be said of all of them, to be sure, but influential figures like Petrarch and Erasmus profoundly distrusted modern experience. They thus introduced a bias that effectively set their successors in a rigid posture of finding essential humanity in the disembodied realm of ideas, abstracted from social evolution and historical transformations.

A related aspect of the problem is the faith-like, ideological rigidity many critics of capitalism share. In a memoir of the 1960s, Irving Howe recalls that the young members of Students for a Democratic Society he encountered, like Tom Hayden, were bright, idealistic, and committed. But they were also rigidly doctrinaire and fanatical. One could already see in Hayden's style, Howe recounts, the beginnings of a commissar, "the authoritarian poisons of this century had seeped into the depths of his mind."[4]

Any faith is quick to condemn yet quick to find excuses. It took French intellectuals like Maurice Merleau-Ponty and even Sartre years to realize the horrors of Stalinist Russia. My own experience in academia suggests that the critics of capitalism are not primarily interested in either argument or facts. Their convictions are not always held on empirical grounds; they are often like articles of faith with deep taproots in emotional dispositions. This is one of the reasons why the critics of capitalism so often affect a self-righteousness, a moral superiority, a bold rhetoric that makes serious intellectual debate difficult.

Capitalism is a humanism—in some ways superior to the humanism proclaimed by its self-styled critics; in most ways compatible with their own deepest desires for a better world, and in all ways worthy of their most serious attention. It rests upon quite explicit moral and philosophical considerations. When one reads the founding advocates of the new commercial order, such as Adam Smith or Montesquieu, it is clear that they were consciously introducing what they thought was a superior culture, superior both in promoting individual virtue and in guaranteeing more stable political arrangements. These advocates, according to Ralph Lerner,

> had first to show their audience that the old preoccupations entailed unacceptable costs and consequences. Then—a much larger task—they had to propose a new model of political and social life, sketch its leading features in some detail, develop a case for preferring it, and defend it as sufficient to cope with the shortcomings of the existing order. In all of these undertakings the advocates of the commercial republic show themselves to have been uncommon men, exceptionally clear and sharp-sighted moderns who knew what they were rejecting and why.[5]

What they rejected was principally the aristocratic bias of the old order, with its emphasis on such intangible goals as salvation and honor. In place of these goals proponents of the new order substituted utility, a morality based upon self-interest regulated by the impersonal mechanism of the marketplace. All moral systems have as their goal the control and direction of human passions. Thus Adam Smith called the market model "the natural system of perfect liberty and justice."[6] Benjamin Rush called commerce an instrument of "humanizing mankind."[7] Alexis de Tocqueville was of the opinion that commercial culture encourages us "to try to attain that form of greatness and happiness which is proper to ourselves."[8] Montesquieu thought commerce would "soften barbaric morals" and induce peace among nations.[9] If nations engage in trade, the chances of war lessen. President Eisenhower echoed Montesquieu when he advocated trade with the Russians as a means of containing their ambition for world domination. Commerce, wrote Montesquieu in *The Spirit of the Laws,*

> is a cure for the most destructive prejudices; for it is almost a general rule, that wherever we find agreeable manners, there commerce flourishes; and that wherever there is com-

merce, there we meet with agreeable manners. . . . Peace is the natural effect of trade. Two nations who traffic with each other become reciprocally dependent; for if one has an interest in buying, the other has an interest in selling; and thus their union is founded on their mutual necessities.[10]

One of the best cases for capitalism as a humanism was made by David Hume. Hume bases his argument on three tenets: commerce improves virtue, strengthens the political community, and promotes culture. Among the virtues fostered in the commercial republic Hume mentions responsibility, mildness and moderation (Montesquieu's *le doux commerce* seems to have been something of a household expression at the time), and law and order. Hume says: "Law, order, police, discipline can never be carried to any degree of perfection until human reason has refined itself in the exercise of commerce and manufacture."[11] Hume lays special stress on initiative and the kind of ambition stimulated by commerce. "This is perhaps the chief advantage which arises from commerce with strangers," he writes. "It rouses men from their indolence; and, presenting the gayer and more opulent part of the nation with objects of luxury which they never before dreamed of, raises in them a desire of a more splendid way of life that what their ancestors enjoyed."[12]

Individual virtue, made possible by the practice of trade and manufacture, also strengthens the state. Private enterprise and a spirited sense of the public go hand in hand. This reciprocity is virtually inevitable for Hume.

> The greatness of a state, and the happiness of its subjects, how independent soever they may be supposed in some respects, are commonly allowed to be inseparable with regard to commerce; and as private men receive greater security, in the possession of their trade and riches, from the power of the public, so the public becomes powerful in proportion to the opulence and extensive commerce of private men.[13]

Industry and trade "increase the power of the sovereign, as well as the happiness of the subjects; and that policy is violent which aggrandizes the public by the poverty of individuals." Commerce begets virtue, virtue begets freedom, and "freedom naturally begets public spirit." This sequence is "according to the most natural course of things."[14] Hume also saw in commerce a more practical solution to the problem of raising taxes. When men work at a subsistence level there is no surplus wealth for the state. In a canny aside to the sovereign, Hume offers this advice: "Furnish him with manufactures and commodities, and he will do it for himself; afterwards you will find it easy to seize some part of his superfluous labour, and employ it in the public service. . . . The greater is the stock of labour of all kinds, the greater quantity may be taken from the heap without making any sensible alteration in it."[15]

Hume's strongest argument rests on his analysis of commodities and the close connection he postulates between commerce and culture, art and civility. Commodities were not for Hume, as they were for Marx, a kind of fetishism; nor were they symptoms of a rank materialism, as they were for Arnold. Rather they were a high expression of human creativity directly related to our most civilized achievements. The argument, in simple form, is this: commerce produces commodities; commodities produce refinement; refinement produces virtue. "The ages of refinement are both the happiest and the most virtuous."[16] Hume makes a brilliant connection between the mechanical and the liberal arts: "The same age which produces great philosophers and politicians, renowned generals and poets, usually abounds with skillful weavers and ship carpenters. We cannot reasonably expect that a piece of woollen cloth will be brought to perfection in a nation which is ignorant of astronomy, or where ethics are neglected."[17] The spirit that makes a nation great in commerce will be the same spirit that makes it great in cultural accomplishments. The spirit of excellence first aroused by commerce will carry over to art and science with the result that "profound ignorance is totally banished, and men enjoy the privilege of rational creatures, to think as well as to act, to cultivate the pleasures of the mind as well as those of the body."[18]

No one has made this particular argument as cogently as Hume. One finds elements of it in the Greeks, and the medievals were quite conscious of the connection between theoretical and practical activities. But after the Renaissance, this integral manner of construing values is largely lost, and never expressed as forcefully as in Hume. Industry and knowledge are "linked together by an indissoluble chain" to increase and show forth our humanity. These qualities, both reason and experience show, are found "to be peculiar to the more polished, and what are commonly denominated, the more luxurious ages." There is nothing foppish or effete in Hume's use of words like "refinement," "luxury," "pleasure." He associates them with commodities and associates commodities with high culture. Hume's humanism is robust and unequivocal. Commerce and knowledge work in tandem "to increase our humanity"; they are the chief characteristics that distinguish a civilized age from times of barbarism and ignorance.[19]

Hume emphasizes, as always, the advantages of commerce for the political order. "But industry, knowledge, and humanity are not advantageous in private life alone; they diffuse their beneficial influence on the public to render the government as great and flourishing as they make individuals happy and prosperous. The increase and consumption of all the commodities are advantages to society." The converse is also true, that "in a society where there is no demand for such superfluities, men sink into indolence, lose all enjoyment of life, and are useless to the public."[20] Hume's argument now looks like this: progress in commerce leads to progress in the arts, which in turn "is favorable to freedom and has a natural tendency to preserve, if not produce, a free government."[21]

Capitalism is not, of course, merely a matter of moral and philosophical principles. The final test of its humanistic worth must be empirical. One has to turn to capitalism's record of performance: In what ways has capitalism made life in society more human? How well in fact has democratic capitalism fulfilled the prescriptions of its early advocates? I believe that democratic capitalism's principal contributions are just what Hume said they were. By increasing the wealth of nations capitalism has simultaneously enhanced individual worth, increased political freedoms, and raised the level of culture. The primacy of the individual has from Greek times been honored as the fundamental principle of humanism. But not until the political and social revolutions of the seventeenth and eighteenth centuries was the principle effectively implemented in social institutions. The idea that each person possesses certain inalienable rights and that an important responsibility of society is to protect those rights was a relatively late development. The concomitant growth of democracy and capitalism added rich new meanings to the traditional concept of humanism.

No society in history has ever supported its intellectuals as has democratic capitalism. The reason for commerce's support of culture is clear: both are organized on the principle of freedom. Freedom of thought is sustained by freedom of the market; indeed, the former is very often impossible without the latter. Nowhere better than in societies where commerce thrives does materiality get translated into the ideal goods of culture and spirituality; nowhere do individual efforts so quickly merge into public benefits. If capitalism has done so much in the teeth of open hostility from so many intellectuals, imagine what might be the case had they supported it.

Notes

1. Ernest Barker, *Political Thought in England 1848–1914* (London: Oxford University Press, 1915), p. 179.
2. See Erich Heller, *The Artist's Journey into the Interior* (New York: Random House, 1959), p. 103.

3. Ibid.

4. Irving Howe, "The Decade That Failed," in *The New York Times Magazine*, Sept. 19, 1982, p. 43.

5. Ralph Lerner, "Commerce and Character: The Anglo-American as New-Model Man," in *Liberation South, Liberation North*, ed. Michael Novak (Washington, D.C.: American Enterprise Institute, 1981), pp. 25–49.

6. Quoted in ibid., p. 29.

7. Ibid., p. 37.

8. Ibid., p. 49.

9. Ibid., p. 36.

10. Ibid. I would like to point out here that we quite desperately need at this time a philosophy of money. Money is one of the great human technologies ranking with the invention of the alphabet, the printing press, and the telegraph (which, according to Marshall McLuhan, were the greatest human inventions). Money, to paraphrase one of Walker Percy's characters, is a great human value. But we seldom hear much in this vein from humanists. The standard eight volume encyclopedia of philosophy, for example, has no entry under Money. In my long years of humanistic education I do not think I ever heard the subject mentioned, except disdainfully. There is something seriously wrong here. I suggest Montesquieu would be a good place to start. He understood money as a symbol of human creativity and a powerful regulator of human conduct. An interesting modern treatment is Alfred Sohn-Rethel's *Intellectual and Manual Labour: A Critique of Epistemology*. He argues that the invention of money made possible abstract thinking in mathematics and formal philosophy. A homology exists between the kind of abstraction required in a monetized society and the realm of thought. It is fascinating to think that Plato's theory of Forms may be a direct consequence of the introduction of money around 600 B.C.! There is an important role for liberal education in working out a philosophy of money.

11. David Hume, "Of Refinement in the Arts," in *Essays Moral, Political and Literary* (London: Oxford University Press, 1963), p. 280.

12. David Hume, "Of Commerce," ibid., p. 270.

13. Ibid., p. 261.

14. Ibid., pp. 265, 266.

15. Ibid., p. 268.

16. David Hume, "Of Refinement in the Arts," p. 276.

17. Ibid., pp. 277–8.

18. Ibid., p. 278.

19. Ibid.

20. Ibid., p. 279.

21. Ibid., p. 263.

4

Conclusion:
Toward a More Integral Humanism

Capitalism is, then, a humanism on empirical grounds. But it is neither perfect nor complete. We need a more integral humanism. Following are ten principles for a stronger, more comprehensive humanism. I offer these principles as a strategy for future action, a basis for dialogue that the left and the right, the critics and the defenders of capitalism might agree on.

1. *The Principle of Alienation.* This principle is connoted, in stronger language, by the theological doctrine of sin and, in milder language, by the liberal tradition's emphasis on fallibilism. The insight in all cases is that man is an imperfect creature whose reach ought not exceed his grasp. The idealist temperament is moved by extremes, is likely to be mesmerized by impossible dreams, and seeks to ground value on nonempirical bases. The humanist knows how easy it is to slip our moorings, how insidious is the temptation to free float far from sensuous encumbrances. So he cautions the greatest realism, based on a keen sense of limits. In his famous debate with Jean-Paul Sartre, Albert Camus quite brilliantly argued for a philosophy of due measure. The temptation to absolutism was, he said, the characteristic temptation of our times and led inevitably to political revolutions unprecedented in their capacity to let blood and deal death. Man, said Camus, is a relative creature; he should have learned by now that to taste of the fruit of the Absolute is to poison the wells of human creativity and prepare the path to nihilism. We must relearn that the first condition of being human is to refuse the status of divinity.

2. *The Principle of Freedom.* Man is a limited but not a determined creature. His freedom is not absolute, but it is real. It is, furthermore, sufficient to his condition. Freedom means that we can deal effectively with any situation in light of consciously chosen goals. Because of the reality of freedom we are endowed with a threefold power: through choice we define our humanity, we create our society, and we are able to resist enslavement to extraneous influences. It is

through freedom, wrote Nicolai Berdyaev, that we overcome the "heaviness" of the world. This sense of freedom, as a defining principle of human nature, was first worked out in the great doctrinal disputes of the Middle Ages. As a result of these disputes, Jacques Maritain noted in his important study of humanism, it was established that man "is free when he acts under divine grace; and that, interiorly vivified by it, he freely posits good and meritorious acts; and that he is alone responsible for the evil that he does; and that his freedom confers on him in the world a role and initiatives of unimaginable importance."[1]

3. *The Principle of Rationality.* Reason has quite consistently been claimed in the humanistic tradition as the crowning glory of man. The medieval thinker Berengar of Tours in the eleventh century gave one classic expression of this tradition when he wrote: "It is part of courage to have recourse to dialectic in all things, for recourse to dialectic is recourse to reason, and he who does not avail himself of reason in all things abandons his chief honor since by virtue of reason he was made in the image of God."[2] It is always possible to overestimate the powers of rationality, to fall into some form of rationalism. Reason, like all human powers, is limited. It is not "pure" reason or merely cognitive, as some philosophers would have it, but a commodious principle that is compatible with and may on occasion be inferior to other human powers, such as the will or the emotions. The claims of rationality inform, but are tempered and hedged by the claims of nature, morality, society, tradition, and religion.

Whence five further principles of humanism.

4. *The Principle of Naturalism.* This principle implies the primacy of the natural over the human, a continuity between the two, the intelligibility of nature and its allegorical power. Humanism must have a cosmic setting, indeed a cosmic consciousness. Nature has primacy in two senses: it is the genitive power of all things, and it is the ground of human rationality, containing what the ancients called the *rationes seminales*—those seeds of intelligence sprinkled generously throughout creation. This second sense was communicated traditionally by theories of natural law and by the sacramental theologies; in modern times that task has fallen almost exclusively to the natural sciences. Scientific method, as an illustrious expression of the principle of rationality, reinforces our community with nature. Any humanism that is antiscientific is prima facie a deficient humanism. This stricture applies particularly to the idealistic humanism expounded by the critics of capitalism.

5. *The Principle of Morality.* A robust humanism must exhibit a keen moral sensitivity. Humanism is fundamentally a moral concept in that it is oriented toward an ethical ideal and toward a moral payoff. Ideas and action form a seamless web. "Morals equip learning" is a theme that runs from Socrates through the Romans Quintilian and Seneca to the medieval moralists. One of the greatest of these, John of Salisbury, taught that any philosophy which fails to guide conduct will fail to bear its finest fruit. Morality is, he said, the "most excellent part" of philosophy. The greatest philosophies are those that aim at action; the most powerful ideas are those that find their way into the practical domain.

6. *The Principle of Society.* This is a specific instance of the principle of morality. To say that man is a moral being is to say that he is a social being. Civic virtue and a public consciousness are natural and necessary outcomes of humanism. The citizen-thinker is one of the highest humanistic ideals. In one register humanism bids us to be mindful of the eternal truths; in another, it urges us to attend to the arena of our social activity where truth is most often fragmented, emergent, dark. It is the signal merit of the social sciences to have extended and concretized significantly the patrimony of humanism. Emile Durkheim and Max Weber, Karl Marx and Sigmund Freud, Daniel Bell and Talcott Parsons are now permanently enshrined in the pantheon of humanistic thinkers. They have taught us new modes of inquiry and a new quality of vision. Above all, they have taught us to look seriously at the world about us. Humanists who cut themselves off from these vital disciplines do themselves much harm.

7. *The Principle of Tradition.* We are all born into a society shaped by the record of human choices. To know how best to act we must know how (and why) our forebears acted. Thus, I have long argued that the primary responsibility of liberal education is to form a cultural memory.[3] It should impart a dramatic sense of the accomplishments of the greatest minds, the greatest artists, and the greatest leaders. The premier assumption of liberal education is that it is intrinsically worthwhile to know the great ideas that shaped the past and that shape us. This assumption does not deny the importance of new knowledge and recent discoveries (the natural and social sciences). But once the Antaeus connection to our history is broken we float aimlessly in a false element and are easily crushed. John Henry Newman made the point clearly in his *Idea of a University:*

> The truly great intellect is one which takes a connected view
> of the old and the new, past and present, far and near, and

which has an insight into the influence of all these on one another without which there is no whole, no center. The truly great intellects possess knowledge, not only of things, but of their mutual relations.[4]

8. *The Principle of Religion.* Human experience shows forth a sacral dimension—a thrust toward the transcendent, the mystical, the mysterious. Humanists must affirm this universal tendency of the human spirit. Some modern forms of humanism are rather strident in their rejection of the religious. One thinks, for example, of the secular humanism propagated by Corliss Lamont and others. This life is all there is, says Lamont, and it is enough. To which one must respond: there is not enough evidence to support the first part of that proposition, and the second part is manifestly false. The human impulse is to expand the limits of the purely natural. Lamont and those who share his views do not do the cause of humanism any favor when they lumber it with atheism. In *Utilitarianism,* one of the foundation documents of secular humanism, John Stuart Mill was much more flexible. He put forth the principle that human actions are right insofar as they promote happiness and wrong insofar as they promote the reverse of happiness. When some of his readers objected that this was a godless doctrine, Mill answered that it all depends on how we think of God. If it is true that "God desires above all things the happiness of his creatures, and that this was his purpose in their creation, utility is not only not a godless doctrine, but more profoundly religious than any other."[5]

Two other principles will complete my taxonomy.

9. *The Principle of Creativity.* Authentic humanism is neither exclusive nor condemnatory. Nothing human is foreign to it. Humanism suffered a serious setback in the Renaissance when Petrarch, Erasmus, and other luminaries took a hostile attitude toward modern values. Petrarch was particularly vitriolic against science. Following their lead many humanists, like the critics of capitalism, became abstract and starchy. Secular humanism errs in a similar fashion. Both are equally exclusionary and uncreative. The principle of creativity disposes us to welcome the new, to reshape the materials of existence, to seek out original patterns of meaning. Nietzsche is perhaps the greatest philosopher of creativity in modern times. He, better than others, understood the basic human need to fictionalize our experience, to express ourselves creatively, to exert our powers in the direction of transcendence and excellence. Nietzsche saw the existential problem as the release of energy and the design of experience. How can the Dionysian forces that churn and boil within us

be given fitting shapes? Our knowledge and our values are the result of the creative annexation we make of our deepest human energies.

10. *The Principle of Subjectivity.* Sound humanism rests upon belief in the supremacy of the self as the locus and generator of values. This principle includes Mill's emphasis on individualism and self-regarding actions; it draws from Kant's notion of the autonomy of the self as the ground of moral action; it has much in common with Kierkegaard's articulation of the principle of subjectivity. "The mode of apprehension of the truth," said Kierkegaard, "is precisely the truth."[6] Quarrel as we might with the epistemology of this assertion, we cannot deny its great humanistic import. Kierkegaard's self has the following traits: originality, inwardness, a capacity for hard choices, a sense of ultimacy, fearlessness before the absurd, and great powers of appropriation—that is, the power to make truth one's own, to stamp reality with the impress of one's personality.

Our sense of self has undergone many metamorphoses in modern times—from the extremes of romantic affirmation to forlorn negations. Modernity, in one of its definitions, is a denial of fixity. Much energy has been expended in quest of the authentic self; the goal of greater, more intense states of consciousness on the horizon of all our activities lures us through tempestuous waters. What is lacking in these furious attempts to scale new heights of consciousness is the sense of centeredness that a wider historical perspective would provide. Socrates first set forth the idea of the centered self, one solidly rooted in a realistic sense of its own possibilities. The self has legitimate supremacy but not absolute supremacy, for that attribute pertains to divinity. The self has legitimate autonomy, but is not isolated from ties with nature, from the formative powers of society, or from the bonds of tradition. Our modern efforts to find ourselves will founder unless this wider perspective guides us.

The foregoing is an outline of a philosophy of humanism that might serve as a standard against which the various claims to humanism can be measured. The conservative critics of capitalism fail rather conspicuously with respect to the principles of alienation, naturalism, society, and especially creativity. The socialist critics might score rather well on the principles of morality and society, whereas capitalism might get low marks on the principles of rationality and tradition. Yet, socialism is woefully deficient with regard to the principles of alienation, freedom, often religion, and subjectivity. Overall, democratic capitalism would fare best on this scale and is particularly strong when measured against the principles of alienation, freedom, creativity, and subjectivity. The argument from freedom alone is convincing.

Even so, there are no grounds for complacency. Capitalism is a flawed ideal, facing serious problems from both within and without. Capitalism lurches from crisis to crisis, often tottering on the brink of disaster like humanity itself. If there were a better system I would gladly welcome it. But capitalism, like democracy, appears to be the worst system until we compare it with the alternatives. A carping traditionalism is no answer to either our moral or our economic problems. Socialism so often fails as an economic system and is a dubious moral ideal. There is one sense, however, in which I grant that socialism is superior, in somewhat the same manner that celibacy is said to be superior to marriage. Both are counsels to perfection. And just as celibacy works for a few in well-defined religious contexts, socialism also works for a few in limited contexts. Interestingly, the most successful experiments in economic socialism have been in monasteries. But monasteries are not liberal societies. Not many of us are perfect, or aspire to be, or even know what perfection is. Democratic capitalism reflects the human condition; it is for the many who are trying to better themselves in this world in an incremental and melioristic way.

The most serious problem facing democratic capitalism is the erosion of its moral base. A major reason for this is the failure of mainstream humanists to contribute to that base. The most hopeful sign I see is the expansion of capitalism to Far Eastern countries. It is no secret that economic dynamism has shifted to what economists call the Pacific Complex. It may be that the Oriental countries will furnish the strong moral-cultural component that the West is in the process of squandering. Democratic capitalism without a supporting morality is a contradiction in terms. If we cannot supply that morality, perhaps others will.

Notes

1. Jacques Maritain, *Integral Humanism* (Notre Dame, Ind.: University of Notre Dame Press, 1973), p. 11.
2. Quoted in Armand A. Maurer, *Medieval Philosophy* (New York: Random House, 1962), p. 48.
3. See, for example, my "Reforming the Liberal Arts," in *Commonweal*, February 2, 1979, pp. 42–48.
4. John Henry Newman, *The Idea of a University* (London: Basil Montagu Pickering, 1873), p. 134.
5. Mill, *Utilitarianism*, p. 28.
6. Soren Kierkegaard, "Concluding Unscientific Postscript," in *A Kierkegaard Anthology*, ed. Robert Bretall (New York: Random House, 1946), p. 227 and *passim*.

The Spirit of Democratic Capitalism

MICHAEL NOVAK

Novak draws from American experience the powerful moral and spiritual principles that lie at the heart of democratic capitalism in reaffirming the vision of a good and free society.

"The most remarkable and original treatise on the roots of modern capitalism to be published in many years . . . the first contemporary work of theology to look favorably on democratic capitalism."   *Wall Street Journal*
Co-published with Simon & Schuster
433 pp./1982/cloth 0–671–43154–4 $19.95

A Muslim's Reflections on Democratic Capitalism

MUHAMMAD ABDUL-RAUF

The author compares the moral and cultural resources of Islam with those of Western Judaism and Christianity in the field of political economy.

"Renews the promise of dialogue among Judaism, Christianity, and Islam, and shows how the great religions of monotheism can and should talk with one another. . . . A landmark."   *Professor Jacob Neusner, Brown University*
74 pp./1984/paper 3537–X $4.95

Liberation South, Liberation North

MICHAEL NOVAK, editor

North and South America were discovered at about the same time; yet they have from the beginning followed divergent philosophical and theological paths that have profoundly affected their development. Essayists examine the recent Latin "liberation theology" and the earlier "natural system of liberty" of the North, studying the two Americas both empirically and in their philosophical or theological predispositions.
99 pp./1981/paper 3464–0 $4.25

Toward a Theology of the Corporation

MICHAEL NOVAK

Novak describes the political and moral-cultural systems on which corporations depend for their existence and shows that the corporation has goals and requirements beyond those of the economic system alone. He argues that corporate life is related to high moral-cultural ideals, in the light of which the conduct of corporations may be held to scrupulous account.
56 pp./1981/paper 3432–2 $4.25

The American Vision: An Essay on the Future of Democratic Capitalism

MICHAEL NOVAK

Novak explores the links within the three-in-one American system—the political, economic, and cultural systems that constitute liberal democratic capital-

ism. He offers original insights into the experiences of liberty, equality, and fraternity under democratic capitalism and the competition between the business elite and the "new class" and presents a strategy for a spirited intellectual offensive on the part of democratic capitalism.
60 pp./1978/paper 3324-5 $4.25

The Dream of Christian Socialism:
An Essay on Its European Origins

BERNARD MURCHLAND

Murchland provides background for the current debate on the religious merits of competing political and economic systems.

"A sympathetic and scholarly presentation of those in the nineteenth century who thought socialism would solve the imperfections of capitalism."
St. Croix (Minn.) Review

74 pp./1982/paper 3470-5 $4.25

• *Mail orders for publications to:* AMERICAN ENTERPRISE INSTITUTE, 1150 Seventeenth Street, N.W., Washington, D.C. 20036 • *For postage and handling, add 10 percent of total; minimum charge $2, maximum $10* • *For information on orders, or to expedite service, call toll free 800-424-2873* • *When ordering by International Standard Book Number, please use the AEI prefix—0-8447* • *Prices subject to change without notice* • *Payable in U.S. currency only*

AEI ASSOCIATES PROGRAM

The American Enterprise Institute invites your participation in the competition of ideas through its AEI Associates Program. This program has two objectives: (1) to extend public familiarity with contemporary issues; and (2) to increase research on these issues and disseminate the results to policy makers, the academic community, journalists, and others who help shape public attitudes. The areas studied by AEI include Economic Policy, Education Policy, Energy Policy, Fiscal Policy, Government Regulation, Health Policy, International Programs, Legal Policy, National Defense Studies, Political and Social Processes, and Religion, Philosophy, and Public Policy. For the $39 annual fee, Associates receive
- a subscription to *Memorandum*, the newsletter on all AEI activities
- the AEI publications catalog and all supplements
- a 30 percent discount on all AEI books
- a 40 percent discount for certain seminars on key issues
- subscriptions to two of the following publications: *Public Opinion*, a bimonthly magazine exploring trends and implications of public opinion on social and public policy questions; *Regulation*, a bimonthly journal examining all aspects of government regulation of society; and *AEI Economist*, a monthly newsletter analyzing current economic issues and evaluating future trends (or for all three publications, send an additional $12).

Call 202/862-6446 or write:　　　AMERICAN ENTERPRISE INSTITUTE
1150 Seventeenth Street, N.W., Suite 301, Washington, D.C. 20036